Matilde Callari Galli (Ed.)

Contemporary Nomadisms

Freiburger Sozialanthropologische Studien

herausgegeben von

Christian Giordano (Universität Fribourg, Schweiz)

in Verbindung mit

Edouard Conte (Universität Bern),
Dobrinka Kostova (Bulgarische Akademie der Wissenschaften, Sofia),
Véronique Pache Huber (Universität Fribourg, Schweiz),
Klaus Roth (Universität München),
François Rüegg (Universität Fribourg, Schweiz)

Band 12

LIT

Matilde Callari Galli (Ed.)

Contemporary Nomadisms

Relations between Local Communities,
Nation-states and Global Cultural Flows

Contributors:
M. Callari Galli, Z. A. Franceschi,
I. G. Pazzagli, B. Riccio, L. Urru

LIT

Gedruckt auf alterungsbeständigem Werkdruckpapier entsprechend
ANSI Z3948   DIN ISO 9706

Published with the support of the University of Fribourg

Bibliographic information published by the Deutsche Nationalbibliothek
The Deutsche Nationalbibliothek lists this publication in the Deutsche
Nationalbibliografie; detailed bibliographic data are available in the Internet at
http://dnb.d-nb.de.

ISBN 978-3-03735-004-1 (Schweiz)
ISBN 978-3-8258-9712-3 (Deutschland)

© LIT VERLAG GmbH & Co. KG Wien,
Zweigniederlassung Zürich 2007
Dufourstr. 31
CH-8008 Zürich
Tel. +41 (0) 44-251 75 05
Fax +41 (0) 44-251 75 06
e-Mail: zuerich@lit-verlag.ch
http://www.lit-verlag.ch

LIT VERLAG Dr. W. Hopf
Berlin
Chausseestr. 128 – 129
D-10115 Berlin

Auslieferung:
Deutschland: LIT Verlag Fresnostr. 2, D-48159 Münster
Tel. +49 (0) 2 51/620 32 - 22, Fax +49 (0) 2 51/922 60 99, e-Mail: vertrieb@lit-verlag.de

Distributed in the UK by: Global Book Marketing, 99B Wallis Rd, London, E9 5LN
Phone: +44 (0) 20 8533 5800 – Fax: +44 (0) 1600 775 663
http://www.centralbooks.co.uk/acatalog/search.html

Distributed in North America by:

Transaction Publishers
New Brunswick (U.S.A.) and London (U.K.)

Transaction Publishers
Rutgers University
35 Berrue Circle
Piscataway, NJ 08854

Phone: +1 (732) 445 - 2280
Fax: + 1 (732) 445 - 3138
for orders (U. S. only):
toll free (888) 999 - 6778
e-mail:
orders@transactionspub.com

Contents

Matilde Callari Galli
Introduction: Nomadic Ethnography   7

Matilde Callari Galli
The Nomadisms of Contemporariness   13

Luigi Urru
Sometimes They Come Back.
Western-Japanese Phantasms and Nomadic Wanderings   35

Zelda Alice Franceschi
Cultural Memory and Identity Construction in a European and
Extra-European context at the beginning of the XX century. A Life Story   53

Bruno Riccio
Transnational Migrations: the Decline of the Nation State?
Anthropological Reflections   75

Ivo Giuseppe Pazzagli
Humanitarian Contexts and Emergent Peripheries:
International Cooperation and Contemporary Nomadism   93

Authors   109

Introduction: Nomadic Ethnography

Matilde Callari Galli

The coincidence of territory, culture and people has been one of the strongest and most widespread reasons for the creation and building of the nation state. It has informed literary works and wars, uprisings and conflicts. It underlies political science, economic, sociological and anthropological analysis; it has given life to lifelong regrets and yearnings.

Nevertheless, in recent times we have seen that the relationships of territorial and social space are overturned. This seems to have dispelled the belief that languages, cultural practices, social relationships, symbolic expressions and handmade products are rooted, in their origins and later modifications, in geographically recognisable places. In the last decades of the second millennium, both this coincidence and the nation state have been repeatedly and ubiquitously criticised. The violent ethnic conflicts, which broke out in the Balkans, in Somalia and in Indonesia, revealed that the nation state is a compound of different groups, often conflicting with each other. It is more often like an "imagined community" (Anderson, 1983) than a framework of similarity. Many nation states are affected by bloody secessionist tensions, while at the same time they are challenged by local authorities, seeking to reinforce their privileges, and by supranational authorities, such as the European Union or ASEAN, GATT (General Agreement on Tariffs and Trade) or WTO (World Trade Organisation). As Habermans writes, "from a political point of view one of the major ideas which has been elaborated in the last centuries – the notion of nation state sovereignty – has been challenged and it has shattered into local, micro-regional, national, macro-regional and global authorities" (Habermans, 1999 [my translation]).

New forms of international migration, new communication systems, new financial flows as well as new political bodies make up the relationships that cross the old boundaries. They assume a territorial multipolarity as their socio-cultural practice arena.

Historically there have always been these integrated bodies. They are territorially located over broad areas and are comprised of lifestyles, social relationships, ideological orientations, symbolic systems and handmade products. If they cannot be defined as similar, these items could nevertheless be ascribed to a common understanding and pattern of elaboration. The Catholic Church has a two thousand year old history of being an active organisation operating all around the known world; moreover, it has multi-local frameworks and dynamics; many great empires of the past can be more or less directly related to this model.

Nowadays we are facing the worldwide spread of common ideas, lifestyles, the suggestion of faraway traditions and multi-locally based habits. This involves, albeit in different ways and at different levels, the majority of human groups. It has been caused by multiple factors, which are different but closely interrelated: new communication systems, new transport technologies, the real and fictitious movements of millions of individuals. Multiple and often simultaneous reasons – wars, famines, political persecutions, the search for a greater wealth and freedom, but also for novelty, enjoyment, study and intellectual exchanges have driven people to imagine or reach "new homelands". Above all this, there is a mixing and blending circulation, itself global and multi-local, dynamic and frenetic, which involves images, views, objects and habits (Giddens 2000; Callari Galli 2000; Callari Galli, Ceruti, Cambi 2003).

The multi-vocal experience and project delocation across entire continents and, at the same time, the coexistence in the same area of a variegated range of shifting differences that are difficult to define, have strongly weakened the model of the coincidence of territory and culture. In this way, a phenomenon, which in the past was temporally and spatially limited, has been transformed into a worldwide one. It has – as a model, or at least as a life chance –above all provided linkages, information and mobility to human beings as a whole, while once they were set aside for elite groups only. David Morley and Kevin Robins argue that "not all of us are nomadic and fragmented subjectivities, not all of us are living in the same post-modern universe" [my translation]. Only a few individuals experience the globalisation process completely; most of human life is still dominated by those localistic elements widely present in our age and widespread throughout the earth; billions of individuals see their life chances increasingly reduced by their experience and are bound to remain in the microterritories where they were born (Morley, Robins 1995: 218) [my translation]. Despite all this, every day worldwide political, financial, cultural and scientific elites adopt the globalisation process as a model to live, elaborate, put forth and enforce. Therefore, the differences in our world take different trends with respect to the past; they can no longer suffer binary oppositions sharply and definitively dividing dominant cultures from subordinate ones, colonising power "centres" from colonised "peripheries".

In these very new conditions, culture – both that relating to the field of art and that spread by mass media – has changed its times and ways of production. While it still refers to what any place has elaborated, spread or enforced in the past – namely lifestyles, values, arts, consumer goods and exchange, the multitude of beliefs and ritual practices and social and political organisations – new places come together, overlap and conflict. These new transnational and deterritorialised "places", such as gender, class, age and ethnicity, provide all humanity with the necessary filters to recognise and share cultural dimensions as systems of meanings that are socially organized and expressed in defined forms, and as such, affecting the perception of their own group and of the otherness that is constantly existing and reproducing itself.

The boundaries of Colonisation are still territorial and economic but they are confused, upset and made dynamic by the production of an imaginary, which is not only literary – as in the instance of the exotic orientalism pointed out by Edward Said's studies – but also dependent on increasingly mobile forms of communication. This is the "wired identity" experienced in the international trajectories of narratives and images (Erny 1996: 2001). This is a new world power map built along telecommunication lines (Morley, Robins 1995). This is the postmodern individual living in the "technomytical age" (Wark 1994), receiving shifting and mobile information that appeared suddenly, integrating it with local interpretations and expecting that orientations will change according to various places and times.

Faced with the feverish existence of change, involving many of the findings of Western social sciences of the previous century, anthropology is obliged to discuss its aims, as well as its conceptual horizons, its methodological practices and possibly, its very epistemological basis. In so doing, it rejects both the universal researcher of cultural evolution, universalist anxieties and the specific habits – often exotic and funny, always assumed to be self-sufficient and closed – of researcher particularism (Adam, Borel, Calame, Kilani 2002).

We have to avoid the methodological trap of assuming reality according to binary oppositions; we cannot choose between the non-material examination of information and the life chances, and between culture deterritorialisation and rooted and exaggerated localism. As such, we need to recover that "strabismus" in anthropological vision that the discipline has claimed for a long time and that encouraged its scholars to enact the role of bygone astronomers with their long telescopes levelled at the universe and the clockmakers of past centuries with their little lenses pointing at minute and bounded mechanisms. Perhaps in the methodological field we have to apply a suggestion that was formulated mainly for geographical studies: "to look far away in order to study the man" (Lévi-Strauss 1978: 71 [my translation], 1984; Borel 1993).

This project has no pre-established plan to offer; it does not want to put itself forward either as a finished paradigm or as a complete and exhaustive theoretical framework. Rather, it wants to be an agenda useful for determining research stages, for noting down new perspectives, places and fields. The agenda does not imply having to give up those tools that belonged to this discipline in the past, but to emphasise some of them and develop them more deeply with respect to others. At the same time, we can try to employ new strategies, apply new techniques and put forward new orientations and perspectives.

It seems to me that George Marcus followed this line when some years ago he suggested a "multi-situated ethnography in the world system" where the researcher's password is no longer settle, root and reside, but "follow". He has to follow migrants, products, metaphors, narratives, lives, biographies and conflicts (Marcus 1995: 98–105 [my translation]).

Consequently, the new relationship between the study of culture and territory entails emphasising the contemporary processes of nomadism and the way they affect life at global, local, theoretical levels and everyday experience. This has to be studied as a projection and as a real experience. This means we should analyse problems appearing in their complexity only if we intend to simultaneously analyse those levels, which too often have been given more importance than others since they are supposed to be separated. They are global processes affecting broad regions as well as continents and local, micro-regional and national levels.

If we apply binary oppositions we can obtain only partial outcomes, which are never fully reliable and which pervert social dynamism. In fact, if we value the first globalising level, only the spatial dimension seems to lose its significance because of flamboyant, surface and ephemeral homogenising processes. Instead, we have to consider the culture of contemporariness as a processual and dynamic articulation of globalisation and localisms; we have to follow Appadurai and consider the lifeblood that globalisation receives by the indigenisation of its message, and our attention to territory, national state and community becomes even more relevant. Epistemological criticism has made us fully aware that interpretation must not be the sum of partial analysis. The methodological approach as a whole changes according to the theoretical approach that studies the complexity of the phenomenon. Analysis items are not bounded and automatically identified within past local groups or national states, but become emerging configurations, representing social practices, symbols and lifestyles, which are permanent in time, if not in space. Therefore, before understanding and explaining them, we have to identify and describe them.

This volume brings together a set of essays trying to show the tendencies of this endless nomadism that cross our world, the distinctive modes in which they increase and at the same time are affected by the complexity of contemporariness. It focuses on the ways in which the myriad of institutions apparently resisting them, in fact are opposed to change and all the possible merging it entails. We had the opportunity to show and to discuss this broad and problematic issue in a panel dedicated to "contemporary nomadisms", which I coordinated within an international meeting, organized by the Middle-East and Balkan European Institute of the University of Bologna, entitled *"Nazionalismo, identità e cooperazione regionale. Compatibilità ed incompatibilità"* held in Forlì between 4th and 9th June 2002.

From the new forms of nomadism, described in terms of their tensions and contradictions, we encounter various methodological readings about their dynamisms, which are transnational, global, real and fictitious. In doing so, we pay attention to an ethnography of the incorporeal's modern trafficking but also of identity experiences, as well as their surrounding state and state-like practices. Culture, processes of identification, difference in articulations reminiscent of the past and new representations make up the common scenario upon which the contributors base their analysis and their findings. Starting from the ethnographies of new nomadisms, these aim at highlighting their mixed logics, their changing trends moving irregularly sometimes, their hybrid overlappings, their fragmentations but also the connections and mutual help that they may create.

I would like to thank Bruno Riccio for the editorial help provided for this translated publication and Judith Land for proofreading the manuscript.

References

ABÉLÈS, M. 2001: Politica, gioco di spazi. Roma: Meltemi.
ANDERSON, B. 1996: Comunità immaginate. Roma: Manifestolibri.
APPADURAI, A. 1996: Diversity and Disciplinarity as Cultural Artifacts. In: C. Nelson, D. Gaonkar (eds.), Disciplinarity and Dissent in Cultural Studies. London: Routledge.
BOREL, M. J. 1993: L'universal et le relatif: note sur l'objet anthropologique. In: G. Berthoud, F. Centlivees, C. Giordano, M. Kilani (eds.), Universalisme et relativisme. Contribution a un débat d'actualité. Fribourg: Ed. Universitaires.
CALLARI GALLI, M. 2000: Antropologia per insegnare. Milano: B. Mondadori.
CALLARI GALLI, M., CERUTI, M., CAMBI, F. 2003: Formare alla complessità. Roma: Carocci.
ENRY, J. N. 1996: On the Limits of "Wired Identity" in the Age of Global Media. In: Identities, 2, n. 4
ENRY, J. N. 2001: Media Studies and Cultural Studies: a Symbolic Convergence. In: T. Miller (ed.), A Companion to Cultural Studies. Malden-Oxford: Blackwell.
GIDDENS, A. 2000: Il mondo che cambia. Il Mulino: Bologna.
HABERMAS, J. 1999: Bestialität und Humanität. In: Die Zeit, n. 18.
LÉVI-STRAUSS, C. 1978: Antropologia strutturale. Milano: Il Saggiatore.
LÉVI-STRAUSS, C. 1984: Lo sguardo da lontano. Torino: Einaudi.
MARCUS, G. 1995: Ethnography in/of the World System: the Emergence of Multi-sited Ethnography. In: Annual Review of Anthropology, vol. 24.
MORLEY, D., ROBBINS, K. 1995: Spaces of Identity: Global Media, Electronic Landscapes and Cultural Boundaries. London: Routledge.
PANDOLFI, M. 2002: "Moral entrepreneurs", souverainetés mouvant et barbelés. Le bio-politique dans les Balkans postcommunistes. In Anthropologie et Sociétés, vol. 26, n. 1.
WARK, M. 1994: Virtual Geography: Living with Global Media Events. Bloomington: Indiana University Press.

The Nomadisms of Contemporariness

Matilde Callari Galli

> More than an art of learning, the art of travel,
> I would say, is an art of forgetting any matter of skin,
> of odour, of taste and any prejudice (...). Rather than to
> increase our knowledge, today the point is to get rid of it.
> *M. Leiris, Zébrage, p. 56*

A premise

A long history of nomadism, through hunting in small groups over the different terrains of our planet for hundreds of millennia, represents a heritage difficult to cancel for our species: for many anthropologists, impossible to cancel. And the history of sedentariness, of the "builders of cities", intense and productive of an incredible fervour in innovation and cultural changes, seems brief – a mere instant, a blink of a god's eye – when set against the background of the millions of years that went before it.

Within all this, moreover, it is possible to perceive a constant tension that, at different levels, keeps alive the desire to move, the anxiety for the new, the search for new spaces, the discovery of new ways of interaction with landscapes, communities and cultures. Moreover, the levels testify to migrations of small groups or entire populations, fierce hordes that conquer and crush empires, caravels that discover new continents, of "natural" boundaries continually violated by an intellectual search, avid and ever unsatisfied, by technological applications ever more daring in shifting the limits considered fixed at any one time.

Over the last few centuries, this frenzied activity of groups that meet, that clash, that mingle and destroy each other, has increased more and more vigorously, owing to a combination of factors: an unprecedented population growth on our planet; the differential development of modes of production; the worldwide attraction of urban areas; the augmented power of the means of communication. When we consider the ongoing cultural processes in contemporariness, we must acknowledge that today the cultural dynamic of the entire planet is conditioned, if not determined, by the almost constant movement of masses of individuals. Each year, nearly six hundred million persons cross some international boundary in order to follow the whims and opportunities of mass tourism, whereas hundreds of millions – single persons, families, entire communities – emigrate for economic reasons, become exiles or refugees owing to war or deportation, or simply choose to live abroad, thus designing their own destinies in the world's vast spaces, or again, shaping their daily lives in continual movement according to the demands of their profession.

The contamination of spaces

One might wonder why much of western thought has denied this reality for centuries, replacing it with the conviction of a state of nature according to which our species is "naturally" sedentary: according to literature, social sciences, "common sense" itself, the journey, the move is seen as something exceptional, an upheaval that disturbs equilibria. Even when viewed favourably, it is always referred to individuals or events that concern passing moments, matters out of the ordinary in the lives of the individual or the group. Ulysses, the hero whose adventures seem to declare the restlessness of modernity, is constrained in his wanderings by the will of adverse gods and treads the path of his return to his "rocky" island with rash tenacity. The transformation of the Homeric myth in Dante's journey seems more of a fatal destiny than a deliberate choice. Somewhat neglected, it seems to me, when it appeared, was also the effort by Marvin Harris to ironically present the "choice" of sedentariness as a necessity made compulsory by the will of hunters to abandon the bloody and painful methods of birth control to which they were compelled by an economy ill-suited to large-sized groups.

From the conviction of a "natural" sedentariness, more postulated than proven, springs a highly particular approach to the analysis of nomadism according to which the latter is viewed as an interruption of a situation where individual cultures develop through their long-rootedness in a determined territory. This view returns the cultural dynamic itself almost wholly within the group studied: as James Clifford wrote, "roots always precede routes" (1997: 3).

If we invert the perspective and hypothesize that nomadism and the "journey" are not exceptional but are basic moments in the cultural dynamic, then territory, boundaries and identities of groups become cultural products, and no longer "natural" entities but elements constructed from the practices of the contacts and movements of the various groups in the course of their history.

In the late twentieth century especially, the centrality of nomadism emerges following the contagious development of the processes of globalization that appear to disturb every part of the world. The breathless processes of innovation cause the "explosion" of that meeting-point between culture and territory, which had underpinned the theoretical and political model received and promoted by the West, especially in the nineteenth and twentieth centuries.

The terms that indicate the characters of the globalisation process as identified by Anthony Giddens (1999) mainly concern the economic arena. They underline the financial interactions that link countries that are distant and different from each other, the worldwide diffusion of modern technologies, the new forms of workforce division and organisation, and the emergence of a "worldwide military order". To these dimensions yet others with a more clear-cut cultural character are added, which by their interactions and "repercussions" produce an even more dynamic and complex picture: the growth of networks and cross-country corporations; new information and communication technologies contributing to an "intensification of the space/time compression" that has had a disorienting and destructive effect on the customary practices of politics and economics; a dizzying increase in movement, emigration, and international travel with repercussions on the social and cultural lives of most human groups.

The effects of these innovative processes are contradictory and hard to catch. Some analysts emphasise the prospective birth of a cosmopolitan global culture, underpinned by the birth of "transnational cultures"; others see a huge superficiality in contemporary cosmopolitanism, a clear homogeneity, determined by general adaptation to consumer models that cling to capitalist economic production – the McDonaldisation of the world (Barber, 1998). And beneath this cloak one finds an interdependent world owing to global processes, yet one that continues to produce very clear-cut localisms, valorisations of ethnic communities that appear to challenge the broadest political unities in which they are incorporated, claiming for themselves the rights and recognitions that belong to nations and states; the rediscovery of "roots" and histories that threaten not only the new transnational unities but the national unities themselves created in the last few centuries (Bhabha, 1997).

When we examine this in detail, we find the hypothesis that the world has been pervaded by one single consumer model and that this has led to cultural homogenization baseless and inexact. The intercultural dynamic of contemporariness is much more complex. As Appadurai warns us (Appadurai, 1996), when innovative forces coming from various contexts are brought within new societies, they tend to be affected by processes of indigenisation. This is true about music, lifestyles, scientific inventions, as much as terrorism. In other words, single cultures may reproduce and reinvent their own specificities appropriating transnational cultural forms through these processes of indigenisation. So we must try to "tune in", as Robertson says, with the world life global institutionalisation as much as with the localisation of globality (Robertson, 1992).

In anthropological terms, then, applying this scheme of reference to our researches – which always start out from circumscribed, specific contexts and reach broader generalisations – the concept of deterritorialisation displays an intimate, profound dynamicness. In contemporariness the cultural processes and products break loose from their adherence to a determinate space, lose their territorial connotations, and become mobile, sometimes volatile, always and in any case inscribing themselves in a particular place. And it is well worth following the suggestion made by Jonathan Inda and Renato Rosaldo, to divide the term de/territorialization in two in order to indicate that, from the anthropological point of view, the effort is to demonstrate that deterritorialization always harbours a reterritorialization: "for us", they write, that "means that the roots of the word always to some extent undo the action of the prefix, such that while the 'de' may pull culture apart from place, the 'territorialization' is always there to pull it back in one way or another. So there is no deterritorialization without some form of reterritorialization" (Inda, Rosaldo, 2002: 12).

In other words, it may perhaps be necessary to not live in oppositional terms, i.e. global and local, but to imagine an unceasing process of deterritorialization that invests the process of globalisation as much as the forms assumed by localism (Cavarero, 2001). We are invited to stop using concepts like ethnicity and identity to reaffirm the old myths of premodernity, and to consider them, instead, as dynamic processes that are constructed through the practices of cultural contacts. We owe to Michel Foucault the insight that space, in our contemporariness, offers itself in the form of relations of displacement (Foucault, 1984: 22): displacement replaces both the localisation belonging to the mediaeval conception of space and the extension to which it had been substituted in the thought of Galileo. Thus, the historical time that had constituted the fulcrum of the political and cultural organization of the nineteenth century, with its dyads "development/underdevelopment", "progress/tradition", for Foucault space itself replaces it in contemporariness: "The present epoch will perhaps be above all the epoch of space. We are in the epoch of simultaneity: we are in the epoch of juxtaposition, the epoch of the near and far, of the side-by-side, of the dispersed. We are at a moment. I believe, when our experience of the world is less that of a long life developing through time than that of a network that connects points and intersects with its own skein."

Towards a map of nomadism in contemporariness

Cultural analysis
Identifying how anthropology may contribute to the interpretation of these new cultural realities, still fluid and brimming with contradictions, is no easy matter. One path indicated in the last few years makes a close criticism of the idea – deeply rooted in contemporary western thought and life – that views community models and the attractions towards localism as natural and innate entities. In effect, it seems to me that by applying to them, too, the epistemological principles of our methodology they may be traced back to their culturalness, considering them as results of identity-forming political and social practices. If we accept avoiding to be trapped in the "metaphysics of sedentariness" (Malkki, 1997, p. 61) – which in any case run totally counter to the results of our research and studies on the history of our species – if we do not consider rootedness and attachment to the community as obvious and inevitable, if we refuse to uncritically accept that the affective potentials and identity principles spring uniquely and automatically from experiences connected to the places where one lives and the daily relations of "face to face" encounters, we shall clearly see that the seemingly immediate, direct experience of community life actually comprises a far more ample apparatus of social and spatial relations. And today an increasing

amount of cultural studies aim to found an analysis of contemporariness by placing at the centre of their interests the diffusion of the phenomena of globalisation, accompanied, upheld, contradicted by a culture at once global and fragmented, deterritorialised and localistic. In particular, their attention is attracted by the crisscrossing of local and global, the connection between globalisation and the emergence of new forms of exclusion and inequality, the relation between the transnationalisation of specific contexts and the contextual rearticulation of transnational flows – human, financial, of images, ideas, information (Appadurai, 1996; Augé, 1997; Callari Galli, 1998, 2000).

The new nomadisms that permeate contemporary society increasingly become the privileged and emerging object of cultural research and reflection. Different sources give rise to new concepts or a reappraisal of old terminologies, such as "diaspora", cultural transmission, "tourism", migration, identity: all used in an attempt to explain what appears to be a new model and a new way of living the nomadism that has always belonged to our species. Ever more numerous are the anthropological studies that abandon the theoretical scheme, which posits a cultural dynamic unfolding entirely among sociocultural systems that are unitary and firmly tied to a territory, and would rather speak of "hybrid" cultures (Canclini, 1990), "cultural horizons" (Appadurai, 1990), "contaminations" (Callari Galli, 1995, 1996, 2000), "mestizo logics" (Amselle, 1990), "routes" (Clifford, 1997), not to mention other anticipations that prefigured broad panoramas in which to inscribe vast aggregates of populations, differing in several cultural aspects but reunified by the very fact of their nomadism (Lewis, 1973, Harrison, Callari Galli, 1971).

James Clifford expresses the hope that, alongside the "centres", the villages, the negotiations inside the group, anthropological analysis will also take into account the places of passage, the mediations with travellers, and the spaces continually shifted and traversed. With this perspective, the limits between "centre" and "periphery" become mixed, while new social actors emerge as protagonists of the cultural dynamics: translators, missionaries, explorers, international aid providers, tourists, migrant groups, "refugees", commuting and seasonal workers (Bhabha, 1994, 1997; Mudimbe, 1988).

Yet, one cannot rest peacefully on these concepts. If the "original purity" theory of one culture or another is devoid of all historical foundation, and with its falsity appears full of peril at a conceptual and political level, underpinning the interpretation of contemporariness with hybridism as its sole condition (Inda, Rosaldo, 2002) fails to account for the differential characters, with respect to the past, that present cultural exchange has caused and determined via the current processes of globalisation. Perhaps one should use more precise categories that, following Bachtin, distinguish an organic hybridism, typical of all cultural encounters in every age, from an intentional hybridism, which, by inserting the search for an aesthetic as much as a cultural *shock,* would better account of the immediacy – one might almost say, the voracity – of the current hybridisation processes. Above all, they may enable one to examine the different hybridisms, the reversed contaminations, referring them to the various contexts in which they occur, and to consider, in expounding their dynamics, the role played by the power differential existing among the different parts in contact (Amhad, 1995; Tomlinson, 1999).

Migratory Processes: Ambiguities and Prospects
The massive movements of human beings across international borders, which have been taking place for a few years now, have gradually become one of the most ambiguous problems from the theoretical point of view, and one of the most difficult to face from the practical-political one. Neglected for years even by demographers and social scientists, they are now considered a topic entailing various levels of analysis and interpretation, and which involve many levels, be they ethical or legal, cultural and economic, or involving social safety and human rights.

Before presenting them rapidly, I wish to make a mainly quantitative clarification, which removes or downscales the atmosphere of crisis and alarm surrounding the widespread social representation of migratory processes. The results of the dynamic and longitudinal analyses carried out worldwide in the sphere of international migrations, including both voluntary and forced movements, do not provide proof of such staggering numerical increases that could justify the state of alarm expressed in political speeches, in the media and in ordinary and everyday language. This applies not only to current surveys but also to realistic projections concerning the near future (Zolberg, Benda 2001).

In light of this information, words full of alarm regarding migratory processes from areas of poverty, need and violence pouring into areas of wealth and democracy, appear to be filled with an irrationality that cannot be dismissed as an exaggeration and a useless and false perception of reality. As Amartya Sen has underlined when commenting many speeches on the so-called "demographical bomb", "the mentality characterised by a state of emergency based on an approximate and false idea predicting an imminent cataclysm leads to hasty reactions that are deeply counterproductive" (1994: 71). Actually, the widespread feeling of currently living "a crisis in international migratory processes" has deeply influenced any possible alternative policies. In particular, it is often invoked to justify draconian measures aimed at protecting national borders, even to the detriment of other considerations such as humanitarian duties towards refugees, generous policies regarding the reunion of families and the same respect for human rights.

More balanced views on the numerical flows of both global migratory processes and groups of "refugees" and the circumstantial analyses of the their causes provide us with more appropriate and less cruel lines along which future projects and programmes can be developed. These are organised around two main positions: relieving the economic and political conditions that increase migratory processes towards "affluent" countries, and preventing the conflicts that generate groups of refugees or making them less explosive.

With regard to the first point, many studies insist on the need to introduce policies of economic support in the areas that produce the largest number of migrants based on the growth, within them, of the free market. However, these studies introduce the awareness that they require time, the development of educational policies and aimed education campaigns. Furthermore, in the immediate future there is hope for the emergence of multilateral agreements, which will regulate the migratory flows both in the countries of arrival and in those of origin, based not only on strictly occupational factors but also on introducing in the agreements a strong charge of attention and respect of human rights in both areas.

As for the second point, first we must specify that in the last few years "refugees" no longer seem to represent an immediate threat for "affluent" democracies due to a number of factors: first, the number of refugees seeking asylum there seems to have stabilised and many stay in their regions of residence or on their immediate borders. However, the fact that they lack the form of aid that they have the right to expect from their governments – we must remember that their governments are often the cause of their "escape" – creates heavy obligations towards them for the international community in its totality. If a country does not wish to grant the right to asylum by welcoming them within its boundaries, the duty to guarantee the respect of human rights towards them does not cease by contracting obligations towards the areas which, somehow or other, welcomes them. In addition, it is necessary to continue supporting a policy that will reintroduce them in their contexts when the situation in their country allows it.

The cultures of the diaspora
Robin Cohen has remarked that the concept of diaspora, employed for so long in social sciences, in works of literature and in political analysis, still has an imprecise definition and a somewhat inconsistent theoretical importance (1992).

Still following the biblical reference, the concept of diaspora is currently used in general to define the displacement of groups that, because of war and political and religious persecution, are forced to abandon their habitual places of residence. Culture of the diaspora, instead, implies the network of relations that, because of these displacements, unites vast geographical and cultural areas that may otherwise be highly non-uniform as regards to characters, history and economic and political specificities.

The increase of the phenomenon in numerical terms, its presence in regions very far apart from one another, the interdependencies it sets up by determining aspects of politics and the world economy have engendered over these last years a notable amount of reflections on it. After starting out from the generic definition that regarded it as a product of communities, which, though scattered over huge areas, retained deep social bonds and strong identity feelings, current studies highlight the relations maintained by the diaspora cultures with the communities of origin (Safran, 1991) but also underline those they establish with the communities into which they have been received (Clifford, 1994) and do not omit to reflect on the networks set up among the various diaspora cultures (Haller, 2000). To this end, I think it very important to underpin our research with a question whose multiple implications have hitherto not received much attention: how does one mix traditional culture with the new practices comprised in the culture of the diaspora? Among the people of the "fields", how many are individuals nurtured on the ideological set-up that makes them "reinvent" an independent and happy past of their own, and how many of them, instead, already participate in an 'interstitial' culture, loaded with contaminations and *métissages*?

It is very important to stress that investigating the discourse strategies and practices actuated by individual groups who live in the diaspora reveals that the experience of dispersion and exile also strengthens the bonds with the vaster world, providing unitary and complex visions of both the "local" and of the "elsewhere", of both present hardness and nostalgic regret. Moreover, events that endanger national identity, as in 1990 when the war in Croatia broke out, may have the effect of revitalising and, in some sense, reinventing a common identity among all exiles, refugees and migrants who at many levels – informal, off the record but also official – intensify their transnational ties (Al-Ali, 2002: 25). In Croatia, since 1990 the term "diaspora *(dijaspora)*" is used in official speeches to unify two concepts that until then were sharply distinguished: one defining "workers temporarily abroad", the other one defining, with the apparently neutral term – though full of negative connotations – "emigrants *(emigranti)*" as those who had left Yugoslavia for political reasons (Povrzanovic Frykan, 2002: 20).

In these last years, several nation states have tried to set up links at an institutional level with groups that can be collected in the context – actually ample, fluid and fairly vague – of diaspora culture. We find evidence of these attempts in very diverse cultural and political realities whose efforts are addressed in an almost unitary way towards migrants, refugees, groups expelled by war or political constraint. For these actions, Robert Smith, examining the attempts made by the Mexican government towards developing stable bonds with its citizens who, legally or otherwise, emigrated to the United States, singles out three reasons that can roughly be regarded as valid also in several other contexts: taking possession of part of the financial resources produced in the new country, controlling the bonds that have developed between the civil society of the place of origin and the migrants, and reorganising the national identity that might be weakened through the contacts established with the new culture (Smith, 1998: 224, cited in Koser, 2002: 34).

One problem still not receiving much attention regards the various diaspora communities' actual desire to return permanently to their country of origin. At this level of analysis, it may first be productive to discuss the hypotheses that represent diaspora cultures as a point of unifying processes, calling into question those that belong to the politics of the states and the representatives of the communities, and those more or less precise suggested by scholars. Many studies belie the commonplace that living far away from one's own national community automatically implies losing one's own identity, traditions and culture. Yet, the experience of displacement is structured on the basis of several variables, and is influenced by local policies vis-à-vis the various types of new "guests" (migrants, refugees, clandestines) and by international policies towards the countries of origin, to such an extent that the newly formed cultural milieus are open to a variety of solutions, often fluid and contingent. As Stuart Hall has written, "the diaspora experience is defined, not by essence of purity, but by recognition of a necessary heterogeneity and diversity: by a conception of 'identity' which lives with and through, not despite, difference; by *hybridity*" (Hall, 1989: 809).

It should be recalled, however, that through use of the media, through connections with nation states and international bodies, the diaspora communities, and transnational communities in general, enjoy good levels of political and even economic power, good abilities to constitute points of aggregation that transcend national and/or ethnic memberships themselves. Thus, they are – or may be – often actors and agents of political change both in their own countries of origin and in those to which they have migrated. And this complex and variously articulated dynamic, also within one and the same diaspora community, shows up the error – not merely theoretical but also political – of referring diaspora cultures to single, generalising models, of considering their overall potentials as agents of change, and of giving a too clear-cut interpretation of the goals of their activities.

The cultures of migration
Regarding the analysis of the migration phenomenon, our contemporariness shows profound divergences with the past. Today, as yesterday, migrations are caused by composite reasons that combine, without mutually excluding each other, the quest for well-being and the need to escape the violence of war and political persecution. At this level, the differences with the past are rather quantitative than qualitative since large human groups have always experienced almost simultaneously "the diaspora of hope, the diaspora of terror, the diaspora of despair" (Appadurai, 1996). The pictures of the Kosovo trains bring to mind the sealed trains of the Holocaust and of the ships that transported convicts from Britain to the "fatal shore" (Hughes, 1988). Just as the torn clothes, broken shoes and bundles of rags of present-day Kosovari recall the same items displayed in the museum on Ellis Island in the bay of New York – reminder of the diaspora, similarly laden with suffering and hope, that populated the United States of America.

The entirely new aspect of these movements, these diasporas, is that they occur within a system of communications undreamt of in the past – one that gives shape to desire and outrage but at the same time to adaptations, choices, rebellions. Television broadcasts bring the desperate march of a people expelled because "ethnically" uncongenial to a territory right into our homes and our awareness; they stir our ancient remorse, so that now, as never before, we cannot take refuge under the alibi of ignorance. Nevertheless, even the experiences themselves of the victims and the executioners are touched, partly determined, and anyway influenced by the creation of a collective imagery that paradoxically, in a conflict that rests on principles of territoriality and ethnic membership, completely overflows the spaces of the individual nations.

Individuals and groups are often oriented and driven towards the migration experience because of what they see on television. The network that enfolds our planet with its satellite broadcasts fills all the continents with images of wealth, of a free and happy life open to all, and, however false and misleading this may be, it has been and continues to be a factor that shapes and unifies the collective desire of millions of individuals. Frequently, then, the dream of those who have not yet made their move is confirmed by those who live this experience: denying the humiliations and failures that migration is heir to, concealing from families and relatives the pain they have undergone, convincing themselves that their decision had its own validity, its good reasons.

Broadening our perspective, we see how the entire "migratory space" is overturned by the existence of means of communication, aeroplanes, faxes, television broadcasts, e-mails, and Internet "surfing". Indian migrants, in Britain and Italy, watch the TV soap operas produced in their country of origin, receive frequent visits from relatives and friends. Pakistani taxi-drivers, navigating the streets of Sydney, listen to cassettes of prayers recorded in the faraway mosques of the Muslim world and daily communicate with their communities. Parabolic antennae crowding the windows of reception centres set up for North Africa's migrants in Emilia-Romagna fill their poor rooms with the images and voices of the countries they have left. Even while death is occurring in some town, some village, some field, the collective imagery expands reaching an eager audience that will introduce the images broadcasted in its place of origin into utterly different cultural spaces.

There is a further, very important point that demands our attention and will be dealt with, though briefly: namely, the media's influence on the stack of information and the collective imagery about the phenomenon maintained by the citizens of a country object of migration. For some time now, scholars of media milieus have advised great caution in establishing the direct, clear-cut effects of images, information and behaviour on the media users. Many studies show that the media – first and foremost television since it is much easier to receive and much more immediate than newspapers, photography and films, for example – played a major role in constructing a halo of "otherness" around migrants, gathering them together in an aura of strangeness, of suspicion about their "real" intentions, emphasising their deviances and labelling them all, often indiscriminately, as potential offenders.

One example is the influence that television has had and continues to have on the imagery that has been built up in recent years about Albanian migrants. An excessive emphasis – defined as "a national obsession" (Wood, King, 2001: 15) – on the relation between migration and crime, an ongoing account of migration's negative effects and the difficulties of settling in Italian society and establishing contacts with the Italians themselves, prevents most Italians from viewing these effects of migration in structural terms. In other words, they fail to connect them with the underground labour market and with a corrupt, criminal system widespread in Italy well before the Albanians began to arrive; thus, they end up seeing the whole area of illegality and deviance as the outcome of migration (Campani, 2001).

It is interesting to note that, while this collective imagery was taking shape in Italy, our television broadcasts, depicting wellbeing, *joie de vivre,* luxury holidays and so on, were exerting a strong influence on young people living in Albania. On these images of a land of milk and honey, they based not only their plan to migrate but also the critical premises to overthrow Enver Hoxha's regime. These images constituted, above all, the dream horizon, the imagery for wishing to construct a new political and personal subjectivity that would remove them from the miserable, dingy atmosphere of totalitarianism in which they were suffocating (Mai, 2001).

New questions for new methodological approaches
"All societies produce foreigners: but each one produces a particular type." I feel that these words by Zygmunt Bauman can be a good introduction to the search for new epistemological directions regarding migratory phenomena, perhaps provided we are willing to introduce a clarification: by production, we mean a process that places "us" and the "others" on the same level. In other words, contemporary anthropology totally identifies the subject and the object of its interest, the "us" and the "others", and refuses to identify "us" with ourselves, ourselves as Italians and autochthons attributing all the categories of otherness to the immigrant, the foreigner. In this dividing logic, the argument that immigration is a highly positive phenomenon from both the viewpoint of the hosting country's cultural and economic enrichment and the apparently opposite one that considers the migratory phenomenon a damage and a risk that must be reduced and contained to the utmost, share – if looked at closely – the same theoretical position, although their respective practices are obviously conflicting and opposed. Actually, both see immigration as a unitary phenomenon, lacking in contextual references, with neither processes nor relational dynamics.

On the contrary, the contemporary scenario, with its mixtures of transversality and de-territorialisation, feelings of being lost and exasperated localisms, requires a deep change in the study and policies of intercultural relations. If we intend to play a constructive and active role in a transnational world populated by cultures that depend less and less on unitary and coherent cultural and educational models, we must create new instruments to face new, structured and complex collective past experiences, dynamic mixtures of reality and fantasy.

Each time we come close to examining or managing the meeting with a different culture, we should refuse the idea of facing a locally elaborated cultural totality comprising a coherent system of repetitive and self-reproductive practices, untouched by external influences and attractions.

If I start from this idea of a coherent culture produced unitarily in a certain territory, the problem of how to welcome the group of immigrants pressing along the coasts of our Adriatic Sea consists mainly in evaluating how their arrival will change our culture and how their meeting with us will change theirs. From this point of view, immigrant policy must be entirely aimed at maintaining a hypothesised cultural order rather than a contextualised and identified one.

What culture are we ready to lavish upon them? Which of the many aspects that comprise our cultural milieu are we willing to show and make accessible to them? Which is the culture of the fleeing Kosovari, of the Albanians, Kurds, Maghrebis and Iranians gathered together on the "motor-boats of desperation" by different events, by occasions that are all dramatic, yet determined more by causality than by a pre-arranged plan? How many of these, at the moment of their arrival, share ancestral traditions or are instead participants in an "interstitial" culture, full of contaminations and *metissage*? How much will the abandoning of these aspirations towards a new culture, in any case "other" with respect to the one they are escaping from, not be determined by the insistence on "difference", which has been formulated and modulated in a thousand ways? As much as it may initially parade tolerance and acceptance, inevitably loaded with distance and suspicion, the meeting awakens past memories that the difficulty of the new life and work conditions may make seem worthy of regret.

In fact, this vision of cultural contacts postulates the possibility of cleaving apart cultural groups and products, erasing from our analysis – and from our actions – the relations, the attractions, and the echoes that constitute the hybrid reality of social practices. In addition, today the new universe of communication has conspicuously brought to light the continuous mediations, the intertwining of exchanges, the coming and going of borrowing that constitute the true and multiform reality of cultural production.

Only by acknowledging that the world today is interconnected and interdependent we can then identify the limits of most immigration policies, whose separations, distinctions, and most extreme aspects can be read and interpreted as a powerful means to maintain the balance of power exclusively in favour of an "us" that risks becoming increasingly beset, isolated and removed from reality.

Moreover, if culture is tied and anchored to a given space, a series of general questions arise, which I believe require an urgent answer.

Which is the culture of the many individuals that inhabit all the borders of all the countries in the world? Which is the culture of the millions of individuals who, from the beginning of the 20th century, have abandoned their spaces following emigration, deportation, escape from violent and repressive systems or the fury of war? At which point of its history can a group be defined a "subculture"? Moreover, does this definition include all of its aspects, its characteristics, or only some? What about the sustainability of this concept when we face some subcultures, which, following the end of political colonialism, have become the dominating culture with respect to their economic power?

By opening up the traditional concept of culture to these problems, the most successful analyses today are those that study the new aspects assumed by social change and cultural transformations, which no longer occur in disconnected spaces but rather in interconnected spaces. "It is the re-territorialisation of space" – write Akil Gupta and James Ferguson – "which forces us to re-conceptualise, from their very foundations, the policies concerning the community, solidarity and cultural difference" (Gupta, Ferguson, 1997: 37).

The analysis of the relation between a culture that elevates the other to the state of the self or that lowers the self to the dignity of the other is replaced by an analysis of culture seen as a place of differentiations and contaminations with widespread discriminations, with the achievement of homologation, and with the rise of new differences that achieve rhythms never experimented before now.

From this point of view, an anthropological practice wishing to assume the new interdependencies characterizing the current "commerce between cultures" in its theoretical apparatus and methodological practices, without ignoring the fragmentation and violent breaks that chase each other incessantly in the current space-time organisation, should definitely abandon its traditional courses, place the new *metissage* and cultural contaminations at the centre of its reflection and choose border areas, the uncertain areas of contemporary nomadism, as a privileged place of attention, and thus refuse the centrality that modernity used to entrust on a single culture, a single dominion. And perhaps find its new thoughts, its new words, in "fleeting" places, among the people of the diaspora, the exile and the migrations.

Tourist nomadisms
Up to now, I have spoken of the anxiety of going, of being expelled, of being in danger, of arriving and remembering, of forgetting and changing. I have dealt with places and times, imageries as vast as the world and acceptations of the journey's hard, painful materialness, of real nomadisms and virtual nomadisms performed in that corner of the world that I call my apartment.

I could lay my intervention open to several other examples, providing a less concise, more complex picture. In this concluding section, among all the possibilities, I choose to hint at a form of nomadism that I should like to call "liminal", "of the threshold". I shall deal with tourism, i.e. those temporary, sometimes occasional, sometimes cyclic movements in space, linked, at least apparently, to choice and desire, and that, by their apparent futility, seem to have the ability to be forgotten. Yet, by the sheer number of persons involved and their links with highly important sectors of contemporary society, they assume increasing relevance from both the point of view of cultural analysis and the changes they bring about in the worldwide perspective.

Tourism and cultural analysis of contemporariness
At a practical and theoretical level, tourism represents the coexistence of several contradictory aspects proper to our contemporariness: it is an ephemeral and aleatory experience, but likewise occurs repeatedly in the space of a year and a life. So much does it occupy the spaces and times of both the world of well-being and that of privation, so deeply does it enter into the widespread habits of hundreds of millions of individuals, that it may be considered a permanent element of present-day society, although it unfolds at increasingly brief and temporary rhythms. It brings together and at the same time contrasts profoundly different human groups; it underlines the falsity of its experience, but simultaneously seeks authenticity and tenuity almost neurotically; in many respects, it is a solitary, individual experience yet involves crowds unacquainted with each other in the same spaces and times.

Over the past few decades, human sciences have focused on analysing the phenomenon of tourism. Having become one of the world's major "industries", it has revealed its multiple and differentiated implications, which increasingly show deep links with the cultural apparatus of contacts among groups with diverse histories, traditions, languages, lifestyles and outlooks on the world. The expectations and repulsions of the communities involved in the tourist phenomenon – the community that receives and the community that visits – appear increasingly related to the central problems in contemporary anthropological thought: first and foremost, to the concept of culture with its corollaries of cultural heredity and authenticity, profoundly altered by a reality in which deterritorialisation and localism follow hard on the heels of one another and alternate endlessly, and then to the identity processes, which lose their unitary character as they are invaded by an endless succession of superficial, unreliable identifications; and, lastly, to the circular nature of the relations linking "centre" and "peripheries" in a global exchange of cultural elements that, at the same time, exhibits a high gradient of differentiation and inequality (Callari Galli, Ceruti, Pievani, 1998).

In the context of studies on tourism, the debate focuses on the effects exerted by the different forms of tourism on both the communities/places of tourist attraction and on those from which the tourists come. Tourism, as it has been practised and continues to be practised in most regions of the world, causes violent upheavals in the life of the countries that receive it, frequently undermines their customs, ethical and religious values, ecological environment and urban settlements.

The more contemporary tourism involves areas characterised by power differentials in their economic, political and social aspects, and the greater importance is suddenly assumed by the predatory content that, now as before, fuels the relation between the differences that is managed by the "great ones of the earth".

However, to respect the pattern of complexity on which I have delved on from the start as a basis for this contribution, I must immediately add that the tourists' communities of origin have also changed, though at a more superficial level, owing to the search for the "exotic", which pervades the brief – and anyway restricted – period of the tourist-stay, and has the effect of influencing our eating habits, our objects, clothes, ceremonies and feasts. All this, blending with other intercultural relationships – some more deep-rooted and more dramatic – has overturned our tastes and our very relation with otherness (Abram, Waldren, McLeod, 1997).

Reading contemporary tourism

If this ongoing "mingling" of the tourist phenomenon is accepted, it is nevertheless difficult to apply clear-cut separations and distinctions within it, making a sharp division between "tourist" and "non-tourist", between the seasonal tourist and the extempore one. The distinction introduced some years back by Smith (1989 [1978]) between "tourist" and "guest" now appears inadequate and, in hindering many further subdivisions, proves to be of little use for a precise anthropological analysis. For example, through their researches several authors have proven that the term "host country" actually includes persons who relate to the tourist in very different ways: individuals who benefit from tourism, who work in host structures, or have only occasional and sporadic relations with tourists, and others who are bypassed by the presence of tourists in their country (Harrison, 1992).

For that matter, the problems we encounter in identifying a "hosting community" to a great extent retrace those we currently have in clearly defining a community, identifying its boundaries, describing its characteristics, and establishing its adherence to a particular territory. The long discussion that involved a great number of anthropologists in the 1980s, as they struggled to identify or deny the possibility of tracing a community's symbolic boundaries (Cohen, 1985), has apparently been solved by abandoning the traditional ways of considering a community's presence in the territory, by ceasing to view it as an entity and trying – as with the concept of culture – to valorise its forms of expression and relationships, instead.

Thus, the difficulties we encounter in designing a typology of the different forms of tourism now present in the world are countless: we find ourselves faced with a mass of individuals – hundreds of millions – who, each year, for varying periods of time and in different ways, leave their homes to visit regions of the most disparate character. They set out from different places, reach different places, and have different aims. And that which would appear to unite them – travel – if examined in its very roots, links them to other millions of individuals, to the point of involving our whole species, which, for most of its evolutionary path, chose to be nomadic rather than sedentary. Hence, instead of following the macrodistinctions present in literature in order to distinguish between the different forms of tourism (Smith, 1989; Smith, Eadington, 1992; Graburn, 1995) – distinctions that I find weak, owing to their excessive generalisation and their temporary nature – I prefer to set forth characters, potentials, and risks of applying the concept of culture to the tourist phenomenon.

Tourism and historical-cultural heritage
Owing to the powerful economic interests it manages to involve in its projects, tourism is also able to influence, at times even to determine, how a community sees its cultural heritage. To point out a cultural feature, an object, a monument or an idea as part of a group's heritage, to ascribe them to a definite epoch, signifies participation in the social construction of one's past and casting light on a symbolic universe, while inevitably obscuring others. By giving a specific order to the past, one actually prefigures the order of the present. Exercising control over the past means playing important roles in identity processes. Thus, in choosing a determinate version of a historical event, one legitimises social relations that, by investing the context of daily relations to whose order they seem to belong, the tourist relationships fulfil as important functions in political processes and in the subdivision of power among the different groups that make up the community. A good exemplification of this comes from the research by John Allcock in Macedonia and Croatia (Allcock, 1995).

In the first case, the decision to show tourists the ruins of certain sacred buildings – ascribing them to Christian faith and ritual, without mentioning that for centuries they had been holy places of Islamic religion- has a high symbolic significance and takes on strong identity and political connotations, since it marks an open reclamation of the antiquity and continuity of Christian heritage in a region riven by tensions with the Muslim groups of Albanian origin. It is an affirmation, at once indirect yet highly explicit, of the strangeness of the "five centuries of Turkish might" compared to the current identity of the Macedonian "nation".

In the second case, Allcock describes the "construction" of a Croat national folklore, intended for tourist purposes but actually aimed at proving the existence of an ancient and consistent cultural heritage that would ascribe unity to a region that for centuries involved a variety of populations and was dominated by states, which were politically and culturally extremely different.

Both of the "cases" studied by Allcock are closely linked to the Macedonian and Croat authorities' attempts to legitimise the politics of the new states that emerged from the break-up of former Yugoslavia. It is quite irrelevant that in the one case intervention was on a historical-archaeological site, and in the other on productions of material and non-material goods, such as handicrafts, musical motifs, oral literature, re-enactments of dances and ceremonies. The relevant point is the privileged role that the organisation of tourism – better yet, the structure of tourism – is able to fulfil in these complex processes. On the one hand, in touristic communication ideological processes, such as the creation of a particular historical heritage or the "invention" of identity "roots" shared by groups that are now very different from one another, find possible forms of expression and validity. The presentation of a monument, an archaeological site, a celebration ceremony, a craft product, in the words of the guides, in the descriptions of the tour operators and tourist leaflets, takes on the value of historical truth, becomes known, accepted and diffused not only among tourists but also among the inhabitants of the places concerned. On the other hand, the expressions employed for this popularisation make use of a rhetoric that is very powerful to this end, even while it eludes critical analysis of the sources and of the actual history. Based on the new truths, the symbolic values thus assumed by objects and places, and the new memories depicted for tourists, new identity processes unfold, new memberships develop, and alliances and affinities are reformulated.

Moreover, the dimensions of the tourist phenomenon in contemporariness, its expansion in the various continents, its penetration into profoundly different social groups and classes, its dynamics that make it hard to distinguish the phenomenon's "consumers" and "producers", render it no longer possible for us to consider it as a process of communication that takes place among different cultures, separated by clearly identifiable boundaries. In reality, tourist production and consumption of places, encounters, and goods are part of one and the same process. Thus, the heritage presented to the tourist reverberates and acts in determining the identity processes of those who have constructed this heritage for tourist use, transforms their territory, their signs and their products, but also shapes the way visitors to that country view the identities and the history.

The appeal to the concept of culture worked out by anthropological research is, I think, evident: culture as a range of possibilities among which the group selects some to be used and some to be discarded in the ongoing process of structuring and restructuring its present and its past, culture that in this "operationality" involves and invades sectors of long tradition, new elements and seemingly marginal traits.

Tourist studies at university level
Anthropological categories become extremely useful if one desires to interpret an activity as complex and articulated as contemporary tourism, or, in order to remove it from the realm of improvisation and randomness, if one seeks to design study courses to train experts for its management and planning.

The reference to anthropological disciplines and the emphasis on a tourism that takes into account cultural implications have relevance for two courses of study on the theme of tourism that I have now been coordinating for some time at the University of Bologna. The first is a Master's Degree course on "Tourist Development" activated in Kampuchea, the second is a postgraduate specialisation in "Cultural Tourism" in the Adriatic area, in particular the part comprising the Uniadrion university network.

Rather than reviewing the two courses in detail, I shall try to sum up their shared features. Both courses are addressed to students who have achieved at least a first degree. Admission to the courses is by selection based on the record of study and work performed, plus a series of tests. The courses aim at training experts in planning and designing tourist activities, accompanied throughout by teaching and research activities. To different extents, both exploit computer link-ups. The course in Kampuchea lasts five semesters, the one in the Adriatic area eight semesters.

They are underpinned by collaboration between different regions and universities belonging to different countries. One involves not only the University of Bologna but also the Royal University of Phnom Penh and the University of Technology of Sydney, while the other links Bologna with the universities of the countries on the Adriatic seaboard that are members of the Uniadrion network (Slovenia, Croatia, Montenegro and Albania). Besides anthropology, the disciplines involved in the teaching programmes include sociology, economics, geography, linguistics and communication, with reference to law and informatics as well. The contributions of the individual disciplines are collected and tied together to some extent by the cultural analysis of the tourist flows and the potentials present in the various localities. From their specific standpoints, they highlight the advantages as well as the risks of tourist development, especially when this occurs in areas where it has long been absent and that have recently experienced harsh conflict. The questions these studies and researches aim to answer are complex; from collaboration among teachers and students belonging to such different traditions, we expect not so much solutions as much as hints, suggestions, and ideas for paths to follow.

What sort of risks may there be of destroying and polluting the environment, of damaging social relationships and undermining the traditional cultures – risks generally linked to mass tourism in areas that, like those studied in the two courses, are attempting to rebuild landscapes and towns, social relations and rhythms of life that were seriously disturbed by a variety of upheavals, all of them dramatic and leaving deep scars on memory and territory? How can a cultural and sustainable tourism play a positive role in this reconstruction? In what way can the tourist's encounter and view contribute to creating places/modes to avoid the excessive localistic vindication of regionalist pride as well as the empty cosmopolitanism of a theatrical authenticity, staged for tourists with the aim of making a fast buck?

Cultural tourism is not a panacea for solving all problems and, above all, it cannot be seen as simply a new way to attract increasing amounts of tourists and money. It might instead be an opportunity to become better acquainted with the world we inhabit, to develop our sensitivity, and to voice our emotions. It should be able to improve the quality of life of the communities involved – hosts and guests – by increasing their awareness of the importance of travelling and hosting, of learning to appreciate landscape, encounters, and new experiences.

The development of cultural tourism could become an opportunity to valorise our past, our history, our heritage, yet also a way to participate in a culture able to go beyond itself in order to communicate with the myriad differences that – at a real and/or virtual level – make up the world. On the one hand, by emphasising the characteristics and possibilities of cultural tourism, every community is summoned and driven to preserve and exploit is own "cultural goods". On the other hand, all tourism must be designed and managed to pay great attention to the general orientations of a world-culture that daily, with its movements, its nomadisms, raises its level of interdependence and globality. Between these two tensions, at the level of research, teaching and cultural policy, there needs to be an ongoing mediation, so that the increased visibility of local communities and their potentials may engender new identity processes, freed from the narrow constraints of the past and the conditioning of the present, but open to dialogue and to encounter the many differences that currently enrich our planet.

References

ABRAM, S., WALDREN, J., MACLEOD, D. V. (eds.) 1997: Tourists and Tourism. New York: Berg.
AL-ALI, N., KOSER, K. 2002: Transnationalism, International Migration and Home. In: N. Al-Ali, K. Koser (eds.), New Approach to Migrations? London: Routledge.
ALLCOCK, J. B. 1995: International Tourism and the Appropriation of History in the Balkans. In: M.-F. Lanfant, J. B. Allcock, E. M. Bruner (eds.), International Tourism: Identity And Change. London: Sage.
AHMAD, A. 1995: The Politics of Literary Postcoloniality. In: Race and Class vol. 36, n. 3.
AMSELLE, J. L. 1990: Logiques métisses. Paris: Payot.
APPADURAI, A. 1992: Global Ethnoscapes: Notes and Queries for a Transnational Anthropology. In: R. Fox (ed.), Recapturing Anthropology: Working in the Present. Santa Fe: School of American Research.
APPADURAI, A. 1990: Disjuncture and Difference in the Global Cultural Economy. In: Public Culture, vol. 2, n. 2.
APPADURAI, A. 1996: Modernity at Large. Minneapolis: University of Minnesota Press.
AUGÈ, M. 1992: Non lieux. Paris: Editions du Seuil.
AUGÈ, M. 1997: La guerre des rêves. Exercises d'Ethno-fiction. Paris: Seuil.
BARBER, B. 1998: Jihad versus McWorld. Milano: Nuove Pratiche Editrice.
BHABHA, H 1994: The Location of Culture. London: Routledge.
BHABHA, H. (ed.) 1997: Nazione e narrazione. Roma: Meltemi.
CALLARI GALLI, M. 1995: Orientamenti antropologici per la cultura contemporanea. In: Pluriverso, n. 1.
CALLARI GALLI, M. 1996: Lo spazio dell'incontro. Roma: Meltemi.
CALLARI GALLI, M. 2000: Antropologia per insegnare. Milano: Mondadori.
CALLARI GALLI, M., CERUTI, M., PIEVANI, T. 1998: Pensare la diversità, Roma: Meltemi.
CALLARI GALLI, M. 2001: Dal casco coloniale al videotape. Antropologia culturale e turismo nella società contemporanea. In: Afriche e Orienti, n. 3/4.
CALLARI GALLI, M., RICCIO, B. (eds.) 2001: Dossier: Sguardi antropologici sul turismo. In: Afriche e Orienti, n. 3/4.
CAMPANI, G. 2001: Migrants and Media: the Italian Case. In: R. King, N. Wood (eds.), Media and Migration. London: Routledge.

CANCLINI, N. G. 1990: Culturas híbridas: estrategias para entrar y salir de la modernidad. Grijalbo: Consejo Nacional para la Cultura y las Artes.
CAVARERO, A. 2001: Il locale assoluto. In: MicroMega, n. 5.
CLIFFORD, J. 1994: Diasporas. In: Cultural Anthropology, vol. 9, n. 3.
CLIFFORD, J. 1997: Routes. Cambridge, Mass: Harvard University Press.
COHEN, R. 1992: The Diaspora of a Diaspora. The Case of the Caribbean. In: Social Science Information, n. 31.
FOUCAULT, M. 1986: Of other Spaces: Heterotopias. In: Diacritics, vol. 16, n. 1.
GIDDENS, A. 1999: Runaway World. London: Profile.
GRABURN, N. 1995: The Past in the Present in Japan: Nostalgia and Neotraditionalism in Contemporary Japanese Domestic Tourism. In: R. Butler, D. Pearce (eds.), Change in Tourism: People, Places, Processes. London: Routledge.
GUERZONI, G. 2001: Multispaces: il turismo culturale tra eredità culturale e formazione. Il caso della Bulgaria. In: Afriche e Orienti, n. 3/4.
HALLER, D. 2000: Gelebte Grenze Gibraltar – Transnationalismus, Lokalitat, und Identitat in kulturanthropologischer Perspektive. Wiesbaden: Deutscher Universitatverlag.
HARRISON, D. (ed.) 1992: Tourism in the Less Developed Countries. London: Belhaven.
HARRISON, G., CALLARI GALLI, M. 1971: Né leggere né scrivere. Milano: Feltrinelli.
HUGHES, R. 1988: The Fatal Shore. New York: Vintage Books.
INDA, J. X., ROSALDO, R. (eds.) 2002: The Anthropology of Globalization. London: Blackwell.
LEWIS, O. 1973: La cultura della povertà e altri saggi di antropologia. Bologna: il Mulino.
KOSER, K. 2002: From Refugees to Transnational Communities?. In: N. Al-Ali, K. Koser (eds.): New Approach to Migrations? London: Routledge.
MAI, N. 2001: "Italy is beautiful": the Role of Italian Television in Albanian Migration to Italy. In: R. King, N. Wood (eds.): Media and Migration. London: Routledge.
MALKKI, L. H. 1997: National Geographic: The Rooting of Peoples and the Territorialization of National Identity among Scholars and Refugees. In: A. Gupta, J. Ferguson (eds.), Culture, Power, Place. Durham: Duke University Press.
MARTELLI, F. 1998: Capire l'Albania. Bologna: il Mulino.
PANDOLFI, M. 2000: L'industrie humanitaire: une souveraineté mouvante et supra-coloniale. Reflèxion sur l'expèrience des Balkans. In: Multitudes. Automn 2000.
POVRZANOVIC FRYKMAN, M. 2002: Homeland Lost and Gained. Croatian Diaspora and Refugees in Sweden. In: N. Al-Ali, K. Koser (eds.), New Approach to Migrations? London: Routledge.

RICCIO, B. 2000: The Italian Construction of Immigration: Sedentarist and Corporatist Narratives Facing Transnational Migration in Emilia-Romagna. In: I. M. Greverus, R. Romhild, G. Welz (eds.), The Mediterraneans. Transborder Movements and Diasporas (=Anthropological Journal on European Cultures, vol. 9, n. 2).

ROBERTSON, R. 1992: Globalization. London: Sage.

SAFRAN, W. 1991: Diasporas in Modern Societies. Myths of Homeland and Return. In: Diaspora, n. 1.

SMITH, V. (ed.) 1989: Hosts and Guests: the Anthropology of Tourism. Philadelphia: University of Pennsylvania Press (1st ed. Oxford: Blackell 1978).

SMITH, V., EADINGTON, W. R. (eds.) 1992: Tourism Alternatives. Philadelphia: University of Pennsylvania Press.

TOMLINSON, J. 1999: Globalization and Culture. Oxford: Polity Press.

WOOD, N., KING, R. (eds.) 2001: Media and Migration. An Overview. In: R. King, N. Wood (eds.), Media and Migration. London: Routledge.

Sometimes They Come Back

Western-Japanese Phantasms and Nomadic Wanderings

Luigi Urru

> *Der heimatlich definierte Mensch möchte ein Tier sein,*
> *das sich das Pflanzenprivileg,*
> *Wurzeln schlagen zu können,*
> *zu eigen gemacht hätte.*
> Peter Sloterdijk

Walter Benjamin has provided us with one of the most powerful allegories of the experience of modernity. In his well-known IX Theses on the Philosophy of History, he sees Paul Klee's picture *Angelus Novus* as a portrait of the "Angel of History":

> His eyes are staring, his mouth is open, his wings are spread. This is how one pictures the angel of history. His face is turned toward the past. Where we perceive a chain of events, he sees one single catastrophe that keeps piling wreckage and hurls it in front of his feet. The angel would like to stay, awaken the dead, and make whole what has been smashed. But a storm is blowing in from Paradise; it has got caught in his wings with such a violence that the angel can no longer close them. The storm irresistibly propels him into the future to which his back is turned, while the pile of debris before him grows skyward. This storm is what we call progress (Benjamin, 1968: 80).

For Benjamin then, modernity seen as progress features two main characteristics: first, its endless devastation, not at all mitigated by that wish to "make whole what has been smashed" of the angel-like character that is history; second, the wild movement towards a future as unknown yet as the *à rebours* experience you can make of it – something you get to appreciate only afterwards, when the devastation has already taken place. According to Benjamin, modern times' show of a steady, somehow blind advancement is near to their core constitution – and a quick look at the project of modernity now spread all over the world tells us that he was, at least provisionally, correct. In keeping with this rather apocalyptic vision, modernity (but the plural "modernities" would better convey that it is not exclusive of the Western world) has systematically flattened whatever crossed its path. In this case, the term apocalypse has to be understood in its original double meaning. In relation to philology, apocalypse equals revelation: Benjamin's words reveal the earth-shattering aspects of modernity. In a few lines, he tears apart the veil of acquired images about modernity as a condition "that promises us adventure, power, joy, growth, transformation of ourselves and the world" (Berman, 1982: 15):

> In enquiring modernity through its least appealing features, its apparently meaningless fragments, [Benjamin] reveals the "dreams" that modernity brings about, its secret myths, its well-hidden "images" (Remotti, 1996: 140).

Yet, apocalypse also means catastrophe, upside-down movement, and the traumatic end of all times. That torn veil reveals the wasteland produced by modernity itself. Taking the move from Benjamin's apocalyptic vision, I will however suggest the possibility of a less dramatic approach to modernity and its remnants. Instead, light will be shed upon the inherent vitality of the contemporary world, and the remnants of modernity will be treated more as shoots of upcoming realities than as dead ruins. Examples will be picked up from geographically distant Japan, specifically from the Japanese metropolis with Tokyo as the most representative place. The following pages will put forward the line that the *dépaysement* side effect of the establishment of modernity is double-edged. On the one side, it has induced a widespread nostalgia for the loss of pre-modern life; on the other side, it has acted as a healthy stimulus for the creation of new identities of individuals and groups alike.

People who have taken an active part – as is the case of Japan – in the adoption of the practices and symbolic system of modernity have then become increasingly aware that a plain displacement of the past is far from possible (let alone desirable), their condition eventually becoming that of cultural hybrids unwilling to recuperate what seems gone forever, if not in nostalgic mourning:

> As culture industries seek to reassure Japanese that everything is in place and all is not lost, the concomitant understanding arises (sometimes obscurely) that such reassurance would not be necessary if loss, indeed, were not at stake. Thus the consuming and consumable pleasures of nostalgia as an ambivalent longing to erase the temporal difference between subject and object of desire, shot through with not only the impossibility but also the ultimate unwillingness to reinstate what was lost. For the loss of nostalgia – that is, the loss of the desire to long for what is lost because one has *found* the lost object – can be more unwelcome than the original loss itself (1995: 10. Original emphasis).

An unyielding desire for origins and tradition is indeed much apparent in Japanese culture's contemporary manifestations. Mass tourism recursively celebrates the symbols of cultural identity, as for instance Mount Fuji or the temples of ancient Kyoto, while nationwide advertising campaigns foster and then exploit the ambiguous longing for the good old times, and a resurgent interest in folkloric studies joins state-led attempts to highlight a continuity in Japanese history and patch up the uneasiness produced by modernity.

For better or for worse, anthropological knowledge itself suffers from *dépaysement*. Wherever they might go, anthropologists no longer face the appealing threat of an easy to classify radical otherness. What they come across, instead, are modern, softened versions of otherness replete with elements of that very Western world the anthropologist in the field thought they had left back home. This situation of an all-encompassing modernity has led some to cry out for the death of anthropology as a discipline; together with otherness, anthropology's *raison d'être* would disappear. Still, the author of this paper believes that the business of anthropology is far from finished. Contemporary world's delusive maze will again make some sense to anthropologists once they re-address the question of everyday life in its multifarious yet ordinary aspects, even in places where – at least on the surface – the most outstanding feature is similarity with Western practices. The legacy of anthropology as we know it lies precisely in its interest in "the ambiguity of cultural behaviour, the opaqueness of symbolic relationships and in the everyday life" (Callari Galli, 1996: 127–8). Now as before, the seeming banality of the everyday, those little trivial things that fill life and fulfil expectations, constitute a powerful frame for organising memory and identity, feelings of belonging and awakening, the local and the global. Despite all the emphasis in recent years on such a catchword as globalisation, the old pursuit of local context still retains most of its validity in anthropology, granted that local contexts have become a playground for working and reworking images of the self and the other, desire and nostalgia, which invariably accompany representations of identity and otherness. When modernity, or indeed fragments of modernity are found at any degree of latitude, the very notions of identity and otherness lose much of their strong flavour. The most obvious effect of modernity is the challenge it poses to well-known oppositional thinking in its categories of self and other, here and there, reality and imagination, original and copy, East and West, and indeed traditional and modern. The attention anthropologists pay to local contexts will take into full account the "game of the phantasm" that modernity has set into action with its full range of losses and recuperations as well as simulations:

> La notion de différence [...] est très active, mais elle ne joue pas entre deux entités, l'occidentale et la japonaise, car aucune des deux n'est *identifiable* à ce qui serait son *identité*. Chacune est faite de sa diversité interne, mais dans l'une et dans l'autre, on retrouve des éléments semblables, dont on ne saurait guère s'ils sont occidentaux ou japonais. (Brahimi, 1992: 205–206. Original emphasis).

Phantasm and the work of imagination

Before tackling the question of the "phantasm" – a notion that addresses abstract categories with shifting references – let philosophy have a word on the matter:

> We moderns, used as we are to stress the rational and the abstract side of cognitive processes, are not astonished any more by the mysterious power of the interior images that animates our dreams and dominates our waking hours possibly more than we would admit (Agamben, 1977: 90).

Letting the phantasm into the intellectual arena is not just an acknowledgement of the partiality of rational thinking. The notion of phantasm is strategic for the analysis of the contemporary world in that it allows a better grasp of a number of social phenomena. First, the very inconsistency of phantasms metaphorically emphasises the role acquired by non-physical trafficking in images and imaginaries that so dramatically contribute to moulding our experience in the world. Second, that same inconsistency comes in handy for any accurate attempt to define the nature of imaginaries as fictitious yet very powerful entities. At least etymologically, as it comes from the Latin verb *facio* (to do, to construct), the word fiction does not refer to anything unreal; to say that imaginaries are fictitious points with their mixed fabric of reality and fantasy, selfhood and otherness, desire and constraint. Imaginaries are better understood as tanks where to grope when deciding on a self-image or a course of action – and this holds both for the individual and for groups, nations included. Far from being a narcotic for easy trips into worlds of dream, or a classy pastime prerogative of poets and elites, imagination

> Has become an organized field of social practices, a form of work [...], and a form of negotiation between sites of agency (individuals) and globally defined fields of possibility. [...] The imagination is now central to all forms of agency, is itself a social fact, and is the key component of the new global order (Appadurai, 1996: 31).

Imagination is very much at work when Western people think of Japan and the Japanese think of Europe or America. Phantasms are present under covers as diverse as reciprocal fear and diffidence, myths in the form of orientalist and occidentalist images, dreams of escape into a different reality often tangibly associated with commodities, films, or songs. The local context acts as a trap for alterity – be this a longing for something now unattainable, lost in the past or faraway in the present. The outcome is a cultural landscape thick with meaning for the social actors involved and yet unfathomable: phantasms, and specifically phantasms of otherness, baffle all description. They are elusive and mysterious by definition.

"Phantasm comes under the sign of desire", alerts Giorgio Agamben (1977: 86): most probably phantasms come and go, and sometimes come back – unexpected perhaps, yet reminders of some other places and some other time. Phantasms are go-between *par excellence,* their effortless movement making them unpredictable elements of social life at large. Given their attitude for evanescence, phantasms fiercely resist most attempts of coercion into prescribed descriptive forms. Therefore, nothing would be easier than to dismiss their very existence – yet, they lie hidden in the discourse of the media as well as in the most ordinary habits of everyday life. Come to Japan and phantasm will show up at the Edo-Tokyo Museum (phantasm of the past), in guesthouses *(ryokan)* where you rent a *tatami*-room (phantasm of exotic dreams, phantasm of a lost authenticity), in the yearly celebration of natural splendour like cherry-blossom viewing *(hanami)* (phantasm of a national community), in the public bathhouse *(sentō)* where you share your nudity with your street neighbours (phantasm of a neighbourhood community), in queuing outside a newly opened foreign fashion store on the *Ōmotesando* (phantasm of the West).

The notion of phantasm with its flexible yet tenacious nature proves useful when it comes to accounting for the niceties of a globalisation process that too many observers like to deem as the very latest thing of the beginning of the third millennium, while also praising its non-reversible and totalising aspects. Explanations regarding the emerging global system tend to fall into two main categories: those of Western dominance, mainly pointing at the spread of Western models, or the postmodern, with a too-limited interest in the pastiche-like features of the new world order. Yet, globalisation is much more than a mere transfer of commodities, images and circulating capital from a centre (the West) towards a periphery (the non-West) that has experienced colonisation and still suffers from subalternity. If globalisation were a purely economic event, or a matter of undisputed Western dominance, it would be safe to say that it had already occurred when local systems of production, exchange and consumption all came within a capitalist mode frame. The globalisation of the contemporary world is to be found more in the very countering of that framing: dramatic evidence of a global challenge at the notion of periphery and centre is now taking place. Which periphery is still to be understood as such if it has become the centre of recognised cultural and political action? The paradox inherent in globalisation as we experience it now is that it lessens the one-way directionality it may once have had and it is best described by processes of counter-assertion and hybridism initiated by those very attempts at framing otherness into a manageable unity. Globalisation is interconnection, rhizome-like relations, and the conspicuous absence of a Western-induced world standstill. All of a sudden the irony of all this becomes self-evident as it lies in the provincialisation of the West itself that globalisation brings about; once exported, Western paradigms lose coherence and homogeneity, they live through adoption within indigenous traditions or they solicit rediscovery and nostalgia for a distinct indigenous identity. The global system is indeed far from systematic, definitely so when it comes to considering the situation in the Far East. For all the unbalance of power implied by a capitalist frame, its very imposition in the East has caused "ironies and resistances, sometimes camouflaged as passivity and a bottomless appetite in the Asian world for things Western" (Appadurai, 1996: 29).

Far from excluding cultural diversity, the dissemination of Western ways is paralleled by a never-ending process of the construction of indigenous differences. Globalisation may indeed further existing gaps, especially when it comes to the perceived distance towards the West. Japan has recently witnessed the growth of instances that reverse previous lines such as *Datsua nyūō* (Escape Asia, enter the West). In this case, the role of the West as a model – and the parallel resurgence of Asia – are at stake:

> The most famous [slogan] is "Datsuō nyūo" (Escape the West, enter Asia) [...]. Others, cautious of excluding the United States, advocate "Nyūō nyūa" (Enter the West and Asia), [...] or "Han'ō nyūa" (Enter Asia together with the West) (Iwabuchi, 2002: 14).

Cultural difference is not necessarily in danger of extinction under the threat of globalisation. Yet, if differences look too much the same, the interest for anthropologists will then lie in the resulting, uncanny look-alike effects. What worries most about globalisation is the rhetorical apparatus displayed by both its enthusiasts and its critics: listening to their arguments, globalisation wrongly turns into the only interpretive tool available to decipher the dynamics of the contemporary world, an ideological meta-narration reminding of those whose life and disappearance have dominated the intellectual and political scene in the last century:

> the problem with this global argument is that it ignores local differences, which can never be reduced to local "variations" of a total system. Although I do not deny that the increasing permeation of multinational capital is now fundamentally transforming a number on non-Western countries, I do not think this fact can be used as an excuse for Western critics to claim that the multifariousness of the world is finally unified into a single totality [...]. [...] by ignoring the heterogeneous voices of the other, critics with a totalizing vision of history tend to succumb to some type of imperialism, neo-colonialism, or orientalism (Yoshimoto, 1989: 8).

The very hypothesis of globalisation being something radically new allows for several critical remarks. The power asymmetry of colonial times was a decisive incubator for globalisation trends. Japan, which did not undergo foreign occupation until after its unconditional surrender in World War II, by the end of the 19th century, and in the following decades, had already witnessed epoch-making events, all marked by the clear premise that a new global context had begun in which East and West could not pretend to ignore each other any longer. The writings of Nitobe Inazō and Okakura Kakuzō are examples of how lucidly Japanese thinkers elaborated upon the new situation, although little acknowledgment of their works – as to other reactions to Western influence – is yet given outside Japan, the mainstream opinion still being, as Flavia Monceri critically notes, that the West "represents the final desirable stage of progress understood as linear and irreversible" (Monceri, 2000: 19).

Anthropology and the uncanny within modernity

> La modernisation du Japon n'est pas qu'une histoire de la ressemblance. Il est né sur l'archipel une modernité à la fois émule et rivale de celle de l'Occident. Cette modernité singulière, inopinément surgie à l'autre extrémité du monde, a dépossédé l'Occident du monopole qu'il pensait détenir et elle a pris de court sa réflexion (Pons, 1988: 9).

It is well known that the re-opening of Japan to the world in 1853 was a matter of "gunboat diplomacy": only the ships of US Commodore Matthew Perry could end the two centuries of self-seclusion *(sakoku)* of the country – a long isolation that, however, never meant obscurantism. On the contrary, it was and still is seen as the Japanese equivalent of the "siècle de Lumières", a time of excitement and creativity from which a unique urban culture emerged – widespread and alien both to the sophistries of the aristocracy and to certain Buddhist-driven pessimism. A pragmatic yet profoundly aesthetic approach to the world was established, whose effects in terms of unashamed humanism and art de vivre are much present in today's metropolis (Pons, 1988: 55).

1868 is a fundamental year in the country's history: the dawn of an era, symbolised by the emperor being restored to the throne, which would be marked by an intensity of international intercourse never experienced before. The change that followed 1868 has been described as prodigious by many commentators, a term that was found again in common use in the blitz-like economic growth *(kodo keizai seicho)* after World War II and that definitely contributes to confine the Japanese experience of modernity and social change to the quarters of the unconceivable and therefore the enigmatic.

The Japanese prodigy has affected many attempts at comprehension: "The subject of late-twentieth-century Japan confounds the simplicities of world order, whether new or old. [...] "Japan" appears ubiquitous, nomadic, transnational" (Ivy, 1995: 1). If you look at Japan, the usual dichotomy East/West is likely to fade away whereas you can no longer trust our inherited sense of time and place – your orient-eering ability depending almost exclusively on a zoning of the world set up in colonial times. The fact that Japan has so successfully entered modernity not only casts doubt on the centrality of the West in that very discourse of modernity, but also proves that modernity can rely on premises radically different from Western ones. Thus, the West is left with the mere phantasm of being the centre of the world. This becomes even clearer once the country's re-opening one hundred and fifty years ago is understood to be just the final event of a long development in modern Japanese history: "Les racines intellectuelles et culturelles du Japon moderne se trouvent en réalité dans les XVIIe et XVIIIe siècles, époque du règne des *shōgun* Tokugawa [...] ce fut en quelque sorte la période d''incubation' de la modernité japonaise" (Pons, 1988: 17). Japanese modernity, then, heavily reshapes the position of the West both in history and in contemporaneity, let alone the effect it produces on the very notion of alterity – something social anthropology is particularly keen on:

Japan's rise to pre-eminence is both an embarrassment to any argument based on the Enlightenment project and yet nevertheless profoundly implicated in the West. As such it is chronically *neither wholly other nor wholly the same* (Perry, 1998: 81. Emphasis added).

Japanese society poses major challenges to the received wisdom and theoretical presuppositions of mainstream social theory. To be sure, Western anthropologists who first set foot on the archipelago aimed for country and sea villages, as John Embree's *Suye Mura. A Japanese Village* (1939) and Edward Norbeck's *Takashima. A Fishing Community* (1954) both attest. Even so, Japan could never be pigeonholed as a "primitive society": that privileged object of anthropological enquiry marked by a distinctive lack of written records and political centralism. To add to the uneasiness of handling a complex society with assumptions and methods not tailored for it, was the fact that Western people were only the second ones to carry out fieldwork in Japan. The Japanese themselves came first. Astonished at the pace of change that was taking place in the country, they produced systematic accounts of Japanese society both in its urban and rural settings. Something like a national epic was born out of the pen of Kunio Yanagita (1875–1962) and his disciples, who in the first decades of the past century scoured the land for everything from wedding habits to funerals, prescriptions and taboos in family life, child rearing, work, relationships, and festival celebrations. Much ahead of Western anthropologists, Yanagita – now deemed as the founding father of Japanese folklore studies and allowed the aura of a mythical figure – practised his quest for "vanishing Japan" with the same intensity with which modernity was sweeping away the very object of his study. His work much contributed to the construction of the image of a Japanese past unpolluted by foreign intercourse, the phantasm of a lost arcadia that only nostalgia could now help recover.

Early works by Western anthropologists have also produced a fair amount of tenacious phantasms. Ruth Benedict's 1946 bestseller *The Chrysanthemum and the Sword* is a very successful example of how the holistic ambition of accounting for society at large may result in a paralysing cultural essentialism. While the sheer consideration of Japanese geography – four thousand isles dispersed over twenty degree of latitude – should keep at bay any approach that purposely ignores the intrinsic variability of its culture, Benedict's book has been widely reappropriated by Japanese themselves "to serve as evidence for Japanese uniqueness" (Ivy, 1995: 11, note 20).

When popular culture matters

Anthropologists have always known that societies can be based on very different principles but work equally well. Japanese society, with its peculiar way to and within modernity, demonstrates this on a grand scale and in doing so challenges like no other the assumptions and pretensions of the West, and the perspectives of Western social theory in particular. Some of the uncomfortable questions raised by Japanese society directly interrogate the tacit conventions of anthropological enquiry and push for a redefinition of the discipline's boundaries. Take Japanese popular culture: be it understood as TV morning serials, sumo tournaments, horse betting, a newly born fascination for football, or a longer-standing infatuation for *manga* and *anime,* popular culture in Japan is truly an overwhelming phenomenon. Still, anthropology has had quite a difficult time not only in digesting it, but also in considering it worth taking into account. In fact, until recently anthropologists did not feel much at ease with popular culture – in Japan or elsewhere – partly due to a tradition which considers it either a too frivolous subject to be pinpointed in academic terms or as a trivial by-product of modernisation and insofar not authentic. Only overcoming this self-inflicted ostracism could provide for the recovery of a healthy sense of reality and open up unbeaten tracks in the interpretation of society:

> the arena of popular culture [...] might well be said to be an arena of *negotiation* in which tradition, the present, the future, a Japanese identity, gendered identity and class/status identities are all reflected, reinforced, fragmented, re-created or created anew. In short, popular culture is the best possible means through which to examine the process that is often called "national culture" (Martinez, 1998: 14. Original emphasis).

The very concept of culture, a core concept indeed of the anthropological endeavour, seems in need of adjustments when it comes to popular culture:

> practices that we might label elite or high culture, have, under the guise of what is Japanese, become more the domain of the huge middle class. Japanese women are studying tea ceremony, classical dancing and classical instruments in large numbers and women are also the main supporters of imported Western high culture such as the theatre, classical music, ballet and opera. When several million people participate in "elite" practices, how can we not label them as popular, or part of mass culture? (Martinez, 1998: 5).

This raises the further question of how global popular culture can possibly go under the same label. The golden rule applies that Western paradigms fail to fully grasp social phenomena in non-Western contexts. Actually, there is no specific Japanese term for popular culture. Plausible renditions range from *minshū bunka* to *taishū bunka*, all the way to *chūkan bunka*. While the latter term refers to the culture of the middle class (allegedly a vast social strata in Japan), the other two terms imply different modes of production. *Minshū bunka* concerns the locally produced products of craftsmanship and retains some tenuous political connotations as it is defined in opposition to the culture of aristocratic elites; *taishū bunka,* on the other hand, implies mass production and mass consumption through nationwide dissemination. The relationship between the two is far from definite and allows overlapping and reciprocal quotation:

> Dans le Japon moderne, ces deux types de culture tendent à se confondre, la seconde englobant et dénaturant progressivement la première sans toutefois la réduire entièrement. (Pons, 1988: 54).

Those of us who used to think of popular culture as a homogeneous global phenomenon, a manifestation indeed of globalisation spreading from Western centres of cultural production, may want to reconsider their stance when addressing it in Japan. Japanese popular culture is in fact so distinctive that Western trends, insofar as they are visible at all, are mere reverberation and phantasm and never supine reproduction.

Therefore, Japanese popular culture consigns anthropologists again to the old job of translators between cultures and to the *dépaysement* that acting as go-between implies, as decades of fieldwork and self-reflective anthropology have come to prove. The rather solitary function of the discipline as a voice within Western social sciences critical of the premises upon which they are based – i.e. rationalism and Enlightenment – is also reaffirmed since any anthropological approach to modernity beyond Western boundaries necessarily erodes the pretensions of the universality of the West itself.

> Modernity belongs to that small family of theories that both declares and desires universal applicability for itself. What is new about modernity (or the idea that its newness is a new kind of newness) follows from this duality. This self-fulfilling and self-justifying idea has provoked many criticisms and much resistance, in both theory and everyday life (Appadurai, 1996:1).

Popular culture is clearly a fundamental ingredient of modernity in the West as well as in Japan; still, that does not mean that Western and Japanese modernities equally overlap each other. Modernity as seen through its contemporary configurations hardly mirrors relations of simple equivalence, nor can be seen as a process of reduplication in the peripheries of what a self-appointed centre might dictate. Again, Japanese popular culture is an apt example since it reverses the widespread notion that popular culture moves from the West to the rest of the world. In fact, Japanese popular culture has been largely exported *from* Japan *towards* the West, as well as towards other areas, since at least the Seventies, as any TV cartoon show fan knows only too well. Its success in East and South-East Asia has been so wild and pervasive that

> many youth feel a more intensive sympathy with the romance in Japanese TV dramas, or with the latest fashion, trendy popular music styles, or the gossip about Japanese idols than they do with the American counterparts that have long dominated the world youth culture (Iwabuchi, 2002: 2).

As for Europe, Pokémon is hugely popular among children, DJ-Krush and Ryuichi Sakamoto have reached brand-name status among clubbers and lounge-music lovers, Miyazaki Hayao has been awarded both the Golden Bear in Berlin and the Oscar. Therefore, Japanese popular culture matters in our own lives much more than we usually are keen to admit and is a rather clear symptom of the polycentric nature of cultural production and dissemination in late modernity.

The exotic in transit

While general opinion has it that Japan is an enigmatic country, academic and economic circles are sometimes prone to the notion that the only possible relationship with Japan consists in perpetuating mutual misunderstandings. Since the first encounter between Jesuit missionaries and the Japanese in the XVI century, a sense of marvellous yet uncanny possession has dominated the perception of each other, as the following account of that encounter shows for the Japanese side:

> "During the reign of Emperor Gonara-no-in [1527–1557]," wrote a Japanese chronicler nearly a century later, the hundred-eighth sovereign since the Emperor Jinmu [mythic founder of the imperial line], around the Kôji era (1555–8), there came on a *Nanban* merchantman a creature one couldn't put a name to, that [appeared to have] human form at first [glance], but might as well be a long-nosed goblin, or a long-necked demon of the sort that disguise themselves as Buddhist lay-priests in order to trick people. Careful inquiry [revealed] that the creature was called "Padre". The first thing one noticed was how long its nose was! It was like a wartless conch-shell, stuck onto [his face] by suction. How big its eyes were! They were like a pair of telescopes, but the irises were yellow. Its head was small; it had long claws on its hands and feet. It was over seven feet tall and was black in colour, [but] its nose was red; its teeth were longer than a horse's teeth, and its hair was mouse-grey. Above its forehead it'd shaved a spot on its pate about the size of an overturned sake cup. Its speech was incomprehensible to the ear; its voice resembled the screech of an owl. Everyone ran to see it, mobbing the roads with abandon. They thought this *phantasm* more terrible than the more ferocious monster [Toby, 1994: 325–7. Emphasis added].

On the other side, Western attempts at grasping the "ungraspable" Japanese otherness could not claim much better outcomes: the search for an allegedly national essence has hindered legions of interpreters from paying due attention to historical change and internal cultural variation. Both aesthetic contemplation and ghastly horror have been regular ingredients of Western accounts of a land all too hastily replete with Zen monks meditating over impossible questions, geishas mistaken for prostitutes, kabuki actors and suicide airplane pilots. In fact, popular knowledge about Japan fostered by media attraction for the cute and the weird does not go far beyond paper folding *(origami),* flower arranging *(ikebana)* and old-time *samurais*. It is questionable that initial academic accounts have gone much better than popular press in explaining the Japanese, seen as:

both aggressive and unaggressive, both militaristic and aesthetic, both insolent and polite, rigid and adaptable, submissive and resentful of being pushed around, loyal and treacherous, brave and timid, conservative and hospitable to new ways (Benedict, 1954: 2).

The ambiguously dissonant presence of chrysanthemums and swords on the same stage, setting the Japanese apart as the most alien to the West, has further stimulated a hard-to-die myth of Japanese uniqueness, filled with dubious references to the irrationality of Japanese behaviour, the homogeneity and harmony of Japanese society, the fatalism inherent in Japanese philosophical thought and artistic expression. What is striking here is not so much the plausibility of these tenets but the fact that Japanese intellectuals and media have first encouraged, then deliberately construed Western images of Japan and pushed them to the point that "essentialized images of Japan resonate with many Japanese self-descriptions: everyday, academic, and mass-market" (Ivy, 1995: 2).

Of course, reappropriation is not a uniquely Japanese phenomenon. Partly due to the peripheral position of Japan in the anthropological playground, it is actually much more common to refer reappropriation to Mali's Dogons and Marcel Griaule or to the Balinese and Clifford Geertz:

What of our subjects' understanding of us? As they do not comprise a homogeneous group, there can be no simple answer. There is a skew anyway. The kinds of practices we understand are ones our predecessor foisted on others in the first place. Balinese read Clifford Geertz for university courses to discover whom they are and how to know it (Hobart, 1996: 13).

Still, the case of Japan needs more cautious consideration since the Japanese were quite articulate about their Japaneseness well before Westerners could foist anything on them and because reappropriation in Japan is tightly linked with the ideological necessities of the nation-state. The existence of a publishing genre on Japanese identity *(nihonjinron)*, which infiltrates every aspect of life in Japan through "immensely popular works written in Japanese by Japanese for Japanese" (Ivy, 1995: 2), speaks volumes about the manufacturing of metaphors of mystery and uniqueness to preserve national identity in face of modernisation and external threat. Works included within the *nihonjinron* genre cover all the range from *manga* to academic pamphlets, press columns to Ph.D. dissertations, and usually "assert with numbing repetition the uniqueness of Japan, a uniqueness constituted as the particularized obverse of the West" (Ivy, 1995: 2). According to this *nihonjinron* outpouring, which is not at all immune from overtones and nationalist emphasis, the Japanese are set apart as a *race* from (or rather beyond) the rest of humankind as the sublimity of the Japanese language (the most difficult in the world, whose mastery is impossible for any foreigner), the lack of logical thinking and indeed unique brain functions, the sheer "relationality" of Japanese selves and eventually the homogeneity of the social landscape (with an overlapping of language, nation and culture most Western nations could only dream of) all too easily demonstrate.

Nihonjinron theses, since at least the Eighties, have been a major cause of discomfort among scholars dealing with Japan. Serious debunking has then followed a corpus of assertions very close to chauvinistic hysteria, and extensive fieldwork has been undertaken to challenge *nihonjinron* cultural exceptionalism at home – i.e. in the everyday of Japanese life. Anthropologists were in the frontline of this undertaking. Instead of merely dismissing *nihonjinron* as a set of absurd and unproven opinions, "a rubbish-heap of miscellaneous folly" as Edward Burnett Tylor would have it one century after his *Primitive Culture* was published, an approach that considers *nihonjinron* literature as a subject matter of anthropological analysis "just like shamanism, kinship structure, or ethnicity" (Befu, 2001: 13) is the most apt to understand how nationalist beliefs infiltrate Japanese consumer society. To put it in Befu's words:

> In analyzing beliefs about ghosts, one might take a positivist-realist position and expend one's energy disproving the existence of ghosts on scientific grounds and disparaging anyone who maintains such a belief. Or one can treat the belief as a social and cultural given rather than as a physical phenomenon, and investigate, for instance, who is more or less likely to believe in ghosts, and where ghosts are said to appear and why, without being judgmental about those who espouse those beliefs [Befu, 2001: 13].

Nihonjinron is not just a quick dispenser of stereotypical images of the Japanese, though; in spite of disguising themselves as purely descriptive, *nihonjinron* propositions serve as moral imperatives: "Not to behave as prescribed is not only unusual and strange, it is regarded as 'un-Japanese' and against normative standards of society" (Befu, 2001: 14). *Nihonjinron* actually tells Japanese how to be Japanese, and in so doing how to differ from the rest of humankind and from the Japanese Other *par excellence*, the West. If nothing else, the theoretical and methodological lack of *nihonjinron* writings has at least one merit:

> ils revendiquent une identité si "absolue" qu'ils se complaisent à la vouloir ineffable. Ces "japanologies" n'ont [en définitive] qu'un mérite: révéler une nouvelle fois le problème d'identité qui se pose aux Japonais (Pons, 1988:10).

Japanese claims of racial and cultural uniqueness, embedded as they are in entrepreneurial and political discourses, are both a powerful tool to keep social order (or in other words, to keep power in the same ruling hands as before) and to justify, even in ridiculous ways, protectionism as foreign trade policy. If you wonder why Japan does not import (or imposes extremely high taxes on importing) skis, beef and rice, *nihonjinron* will provide the correct answer; snow on Japanese slopes is not quite like the snow that happens to fall outside the national border, Japanese intestines have a peculiar conformation of their own, and Japanese rice possesses spiritual qualities unknown to plants cultivated abroad.

A further aspect of *nihonjinron* propositions is their sedative effect on the phantasms emerging from the national past or fears stemming from advancing internationalisation. The myth of Japanese introvert uniqueness goes hand in hand with the willing oblivion of a far too extrovert imperialist past ending in the unconditional surrender of World War II. Yet, maintaining that Japanese culture is unique and untouched by foreign intercourse has its costs: feelings of isolation and fears of inadequacy for the challenge of globalisation haunt many in Japan, "despite the absorption of the foreign in everything from cooking to philosophy" (Ivy, 1995: 2).

Especially in urban Japan, this absorption is possibly the first thing the passing observer notices. Seen through its capital, much of the alleged Japanese mystery fades away, while the somewhat misleading impression of being in a not-too-far-away place occurs supported by well-disseminated signs of modernity – condominiums, shopping malls, traffic jams, processed foods – always available examples that Japanese modernity "has at once inflected, resisted and reversed the binaries of Orientalism" (Perry, 1998: 71). What is most precious to the anthropologist in Japan is not so much the sphinx-like quality of Japanese culture, as made up by *nihonjinron* writers, but rather the uncomfortable *dépaysement* derived by the presence there of what we perceive as our own phantasms, of ourselves dubbed (doubled) by the Japanese:

> [Mais] le double [...] c'est une figure imaginaire qui, telle l'âme, l'ombre, l'image dans le miroir hante le sujet comme son autre, qui fait qu'il est à la fois lui-même et ne se ressemble jamais non plus, qui le hante comme une mort subtile et toujours conjurée. [...] autant dire que la puissance et la richesse imaginaire du double, celle où se joue l'étrangeté et en même temps l'intimité du sujet (heimlich/unheimlich), reposent sur son immatérialité, sur le fait qu'il est et reste un phantasme (Baudrillard, 1981: 143).

When cultures are in transit, as it appears to be increasingly the case, and concepts of the Self and the Other (maybe an exotic Other and an auto-orientalised Self) are at play, phantasms are likely to play their part, too, and the very idea of authenticity loses much of its credibility.

As a recent example, let us take metropolitan Tokyo and the growing popularity of 1DK self-contained apartments among young people, mostly not-yet-married new employees (both males and females). A dining-cum-bedroom, a kitchenette, and a fully accessorised bathroom are fitted in no more than 20–25 square meters, usually with an ostentatious (to Western European eyes) use of cutting-edge technology – heated floors, automatic lightning, remote-controlled air conditioning, an intelligent fridge, a Jacuzzi-type bath tub, an electrically warmed WC seat, a security panel linked to a private security agency 24 hours a day. Since the Eighties, 1DKs have grown so popular and distinctive of a new stage in housing that renowned architects, the likes of Toyo Itō, Riken Yamamoto e Kazuyo Sejima, have not disdained to design them, while TV serials *Tokyo Love Story* and *Elevator Girl* have been set in them and a publishing market is thriving with magazines and books on how to get the most out of 1DK life. The fact that older *yojōhan* (four tatami rooms) have virtually disappeared from the domestic urban landscape, together with *tatami* themselves, *shoji* and *fusuma* (translucent paper covered screens), should not lead us to think that there has been an abrupt change in the organisation of domestic space where Western models have been passively adopted:

> Western forms of architecture and urban design were incorporated gradually [into the context of traditional Japanese cities] first by imitation combined with trial and error, and then by interpretation *à la japonaise*. (Jinnai, 1995: 4).

Condominiums, whose exterior may induce us to think they were transplanted in Tokyo from some Western metropolis, conceal organisational patterns very different from Western ones and only reveal a highly creative reworking of any foreign input. Japanese 1DKs are a timely proof that "the western condition of the family dwelling consisting of a combination of individual rooms for each family member does not apply here" (Suzuki, 2001: 41) and that the destiny of the nuclear family has not been set once and for all. The spread of 1DKs has been eased by the capillary presence of small-scale businesses distributing goods and services. So called *kombini* are finely dispersed almost everywhere in Tokyo and they offer means of survival to the city dweller at any time of the day and the night – food, telephone cards, pregnancy tests, magazines, launderettes, fax and copy-machines, bill payments and cash ATMs, basically everything that cannot fit into small 1DKs. That *kombini* is a contraction from convenience store is as etymologically true as socially misleading since it is just a far echo of the Anglo-American model, a superficial remembrance or, better said, a phantasm retraceable in Japan.

Conclusion

Coming to a full stop in a discussion about phantasms and nomadic wanderings is somewhat of a contradiction and of course impossible as well. But one last thing might be said: the socio-cultural landscape modelled by modernity in the West and in Japan is much more fertile than Walter Benjamin could possibly have presumed seventy years ago. That modernity is a devastation of previous life forms is not an outlandish statement, as the growth of nostalgic feelings over a past gone forever should show. This in turn has led to a livelier situation than theorists of globalisation, meant as a new form of Western imperialism, would usually admit:

> In terms of manifest content there are rapidly proliferating, multiple overlapping features as between Japan and the West. "Their" hybridity is, however, manifestly and stubbornly not "ours". It has a different geneal-

ogy and it generates novelty in accordance with a different grammar (Perry, 1998: 91).

Japanese modernity is at once exotic and familiar, ordinary and bizarre to the point that the distinction East/West loses sharp contours. What is left to be researched in the contemporary world is not the essence of self-contained identities, but processes of exchange, connection, and flow of imaginaries and reciprocal dreams. In other words, phantasms and the unavoidable, yet anthropologically enjoyable, uncanny condition they bring about.

References

(first edition in square brackets)

AGAMBEN, G. 1993: Stanzas: Word and Phantasm in Western Culture. Stanford University Press [1977. Stanze. La parola e il fantasma nella cultura occidentale. Turin: Einaudi].
APPADURAI, A. 1996: Modernity at Large. Cultural Dimensions of Globalization. Minneapolis: University of Minnesota Press.
BAUDRILLARD, J. 1981: Simulacres et simulations. Paris: Éditions Galilée.
BEFU, H. 2001: Hegemony of Homogeneity. An Anthropological Analysis of Nihonjinron. Melbourne: Trans Pacific Press.
BENEDICT, R. 1954 [1946]: The Chrysanthemum and the Sword. Patterns of Japanese Culture. Tokyo: Tuttle.
BENJAMIN, W. 1968: Illuminations. London: Fontana [1955. Schriften. Frankfurt am Main: Suhrkamp].
BERMAN, M. 1982: All That is Solid Melts into Air. The Experience of Modernity. London: Verso.
BRAHIMI, D. 1992: Un aller retour pour Cipango. Essai sur les paradoxes du japonisme. Paris: Noël Blandin.
CALLARI GALLI, M. 1996: Lo spazio dell'incontro. Percorsi nella complessità. Rome: Meltemi.
EMBREE, J. 1939: Suye Mura. A Japanese Village. Chicago: The University of Chicago Press.
HOBART, M. 1996: A Very Peculiar Practice, or the Unimportance of Penguins. Paper to the Department of Anthropology and Sociology, School of Oriental and African Studies (SOAS), London.
IVY, M. 1995: Discourses of the Vanishing. Modernity, Phantasm, Japan. Chicago: University of Chicago Press.
IWABUCHI, K. 2002: Recentering Globalization. Popular Culture and Japanese Transnationalism. Durham: Duke University Press.
JINNAI, H. 1995: Tokyo. A Spatial Anthropology. Berkeley and Los Angeles: University of California Press [1985. Tōkyō non kûkan jinruigaku. Tokyo: Chikuma Shobō].

MARTINEZ, D. (ed.) 1998: The Worlds of Japanese Popular Culture. Gender, Shifting Boundaries and Global Cultures. Cambridge: Cambridge University Press.
MONCERI, F. 2000: Il problema dell'unicità giapponese. Nitobe Inazō e Okakura Kakuzō. Pisa: ETS.
NORBECK, E. 1954: Takashima. A Japanese Fishing Community. Salt Lake City: University of Utah Press.
PERRY, N. 1998: Hyperreality and Global Culture. London, New York: Routledge.
PONS, Ph. 1988: D'Edo à Tōkyō. Mémoires et modernités. Paris: Gallimard.
REMOTTI, F. 1996: Walter Benjamin in una prospettiva antropologica. Uno sguardo a ritroso sulla modernità. In: Enrico Guglieminetti, Ugo Perone, Francesco Traniello (eds), Walter Benjamin: sogno e industria. Turin: Celid.
TOBY, R. 1994: The Indianness of Iberia and Changing Japanese Iconographies of Other. In: Stuart B. Schwartz (ed.), Implicit Understandings. Observing, Reporting and Reflecting on the Encounteers between Europeans and Other Peoples in Early Modern Era. Cambridge: Cambridge University Press.
SUZUKI, A. 2001: Do Android Crows Fly Over the Skies of an Electronic Tokyo? The Interactive Urban Landscape of Japan. London: Architectural Association.
YOSHIMOTO, M. 1989: The Postmodern and Mass Images in Japan. In: Public Culture, I, 2.

Cultural Memory and Identity Construction in a European and Extra-European Context at the Beginning of the XX Century. A Life Story

Zelda Alice Franceschi

Premise

A few days ago, in a political meeting, I suddenly understood why it was much easier for me to be "European" than for others. I was supposed to speak and I realised that I no longer had even a language at my disposal. The Italian that I have spoken for many years has always felt extraneous to me; I have never wanted to speak it to too great a degree for fear of losing my mother tongue, German. But I have lost it all the same; years of loving conservation have rendered it colourless and rigid, as happens with memories.

It is not just the lack of a language: I am not Italian despite the fact I have Italian children, I am not German even though Germany was once my homeland. And I am not even Jewish, although it is purely by chance that I was not arrested and burned in a furnace in one of the death camps (Hirschmann, 1993: 21).

Of Ursula Hirschmann, initiator of the European federalist movement in the 1940s and founder of the group *Femmes pour l'Europe* (1975), we are left with an autobiographical text which is not easy to define (Hirschmann, 1993), a notebook in which the memories gather on the streets of European cities: from Hohenzollernstrasse in Berlin where her grandmother lived, (Hirschmann, 1993: 53), to the office on Rue de Lafayette, "a constant coming and going of comrades of French, German and other nationalities" (Hirschmann, 1993: 111), to Via Cesare Battisti running down towards the canal in Trieste, where Hirschmann moved to at the age of twenty-two.

In Hirschmann's words, the consciousness of not possessing any language to express herself with is suffered through her awareness of being part of a larger Europe. Exiled and deported, the sense of bewilderment that this woman experienced throughout her life as a migrant becomes a metaphor for a "Europeanism of the uprooted". This painful and traumatic experience problematises the complexity of the concept of European identity and introduces several issues, which I would like to deal with by focusing on the following four concepts: *Europe, Identity-Biography, Memory* and *Journey-Immigration*.

This essay was prompted by a number of reflections that emerged following a field experience whereby an attempt was made to reconstruct the historical-biographical experience of a woman who had lived in Italy and Vietnam between the 19th and 20th centuries.[1] Only after several years of work in archives, libraries and following lengthy interviews and whole summers spent in the company of this woman some problematic issues arose, requiring answers that were different yet linked. What meaning should we attribute to the concept of identity? Does it make sense today to talk about European identity? What is the value of memory? Of recollection and oblivion? Are there perhaps silent ghosts who return, constantly and implacably,[2] in the stories of immigration? Spectres made up of representations, desires, emotions and memories, ready to shape identities and mould alterities, dissolving one into the other? Is there perhaps a regular circulation in the contemporary world, flexible and fluid yet systematic, a movement that moulds stratified belonging, nomadic memoirs, experiences and stories, in which *identity* and *belonging* are stitched back together from time to time and immediately dissolved?

Answering these questions is not an easy task; while anthropological strategies have become complex and stratified, canonical paradigms have not only broken down but, as the French ethnologist Jean Jamin reminds us, even the notions of *exotism*, the *description of the other and otherness*, are reflected, readjusted and reworked, not according to geographical and cultural parameters, but to methodological and epistemological ones (Jamin, 1980: 16).

Despite these statements, or – on the contrary – maybe because of them, it may be interesting to read and try to interpret contemporaneity from an anthropological point of view through the "life stories", memoirs and biographies which each of us continues incessantly to preserve, defend and reveal. They may be able to provide us with an approach to reading that shows the opacities of modernity, the ambiguities of globalisation and the multiple localisms of everyday life.

I would like to begin by investigating the validity of the concept of Europe today. The belonging to a European identity may not only be deconstructed (Derrida, 1991; Braidotti, 1994) but may also be discussed once more in the light "of the aporias, the nemeses, the tricks that the destiny of Europe has played with the identities linked to it"[3] (Passerini, 2003: 115).

---

[1] The first interview with Liane was conducted in Verona on 10 March 1999; the second in Allegra on 5 August 1999. This essay is part of the field research conducted for my Ph.D, see *"Le storie di vita nelle discipline etno-antropologiche. Percorsi metodologici per una ricerca di campo"* (Life stories in the ethno-anthropological disciplines. Methodological paths for field research). XV cycle, academic year 2001–2002. University of Milan-Bicocca.

[2] See L. Urru. *Sometimes they come back. Western-Japanese phantasms and nomadic wanderings* in this volume.

[3] The quotation has been slightly modified.

Europe beginning from Europe. Europe after Europe[4]

Travelling through Europe's history across the two wars, in 1987 Hans Georg Gadamer wrote about how Europe has always been characterised by a strong and disruptive cultural and linguistic diversity to the extent that she was forced to learn "the hard lesson of co-existence" (Passerini, 1998: 7). According to Gadamer, Europe's cultural destiny was formed through the differences and the dialogue between different areas of human creativity, particularly philosophy and science (Gadamer, 1987: 15–33). A good example of the complexity of European cultural identity is expressed in two seminal texts by Novalis (1799) and Guizot (1871), respectively. Franco Moretti (1993) and Edgar Morin (1988) have reread such essays and they provide a fertile starting point for reflections on Europe and the value of its identity today.

According to Moretti, Novalis and Guizot propose two conflicting models of Europe, because they present two divergent concepts of the Holy Roman Empire and the consequent birth of the nation states. Novalis' model is that of a Europe united in the Christian faith, a faith capable of fusing very different countries into one. Novalis begins as follows:

> Es waren schöne glänzen Zeiten, wo Europa ein christliches Land war, wo *Eine* Christenheit diesen menschlich gestalteten Weltheil bewohnte; ein Großes gemeinschaftliches Interesse verband die entlegenste in Provinzen dieses weiten geistlichen Reichs (Novalis, 1995: 71).

Novalis nostalgically recalls the Christian Europe of the Middle Ages, happy because spiritually and politically united: the supreme duty of the Christian faith was peacekeeping and re-unification. Novalis, as highlighted by Alberto Reale in the introduction, "presents us with an ideal image, constructed with an accurate selection of positive traits and an elimination of the negative aspects, a Europe unified at spiritual level in a single kingdom. It is not the image of how the Middle Ages actually were, but how they would have liked to be" (Reale, 1995: 25). In Novalis' text, we find all the controversial arguments made by Guizot and which pushed Renan himself to write his essay on the nation just eleven years later.[5] Guizot finds the main cause of the birth of the European states in the fall of Christian universalism. The greatness and strength of this new Europe no longer consists in being united around a single centre of spiritual and political strength, but emerges through being broken up into a myriad of different states on the basis of their political-social organisation and linguistic-literary tradition. The idea of a Europe taking its strength from a common heritage was replaced by

---

[4] I would like to thank Vita Fortunati for giving me the inspiration for this part of the essay. See V.Fortunati. 1996.

[5] Renan's essay was published in *Œuvres Complètes*, Paris, 1947–61, vol. I, pp. 887–907. Here we used the translation by A. Perri with the notes by M. Tom published with the title "What is a nation". In: H. K. Bhabha 1997.

the concept that it was the cultural differences themselves that gave rise to the Europe of the nation states:

> Il en a été tout autrement de la civilisation de l'Europe moderne. Sans entrer dans aucun détail, regardez-y, recueillez vos souvenirs; elle vous apparaîtra sur-le-champ variée, confuse, orageuse; toutes les formes, tous les principes d'organisation sociale y coexistent: les pouvoirs spirituel et temporel, les éléments théocratique, monarchique, aristocratique, démocratique, toutes les classes, toutes les situations sociales se mêlent se pressent [...] Et se forces diverses sont entre elles dans une état de lutte continuelle, sans qu'aucune parvienne à étouffer les autres et à prendre seule possession de la société (Guizot, 1871: 37).

Guizot puts forward the idea of the new and fruitful Europe as a changeable field of potentialities whose character, as Morin highlighted, is to bring together its greatest diversities without confusing them and to link its contrasts inseparably (Morin, 1988: 22). According to Renan, a nation was not a reality which could be described, objectified, precisely identified or easily recognised within borders, territorial limits or biological characteristics; this was the Europe Guizot wished for. The innovative aspect of the two texts, published almost simultaneously, lies in their very "anti-essentialism"; lying at the heart of the concept of nation and Europe, it is always possible to glimpse a "série de faits contingents, de divisions artificielles, de hazards de conquêtes et en aucune manière un principe nécessaire ou naturel" (Poutignat e Streiff-Fenart, 1995: 37). A central element of this Europe as a complex system is the "intercultural dialogue", i.e. the interaction between different cultures consisting not only of complementarities, but also of competitiveness and antagonism (Morin, 1988 22), a prerequisite that requires, "the complex association of order, disorder and organisation in order to be understood" (Morin, 1988: 22). According to this interpretation, therefore, Europe took shape through this uninterrupted multiplicity: its identity requires difference and inevitably involves alterity.

> D'une autre côté, il est évident que cette civilization ne peut être cherchée, que son histoire ne peut être puisée dans l'histoire d'un seule des États européens. Si elle a de l'unité, sa variété n'en est pas moins prodigieuse; elle ne s'est développée tout entière dans aucun pays spécial. Les traits de sa physionomie sont épars: il faut chercher, tantôt en France, tantôt en Angleterre, tantôt en Allemagne, tantôt en Italie ou en Espagne, les éléments de son histoire (Guizot, 1871: 5–6).

In the words of Guizot, it is these metamorphoses, these continued and incessant transformations, which lead to the moulding of European identity. The result is a Europe whose geography is unstable and whose borders are changeable, a Europe – it should be stressed – born on the borders rather than between the boundaries, which, following Morin's argument once more, cannot be defined by way of closed and stable historical borders, places of association and disassociation, separation and articulation (Morin, 1988: 31). Thus, with the birth of the concept of Europe, a geographical notion without borders, a shattered fading if one seeks unity and compactness, those dichotomous differences – such as inside-outside and centre-margin – already seem to be disappearing, while the "in-between" areas begin to emerge, the interstitial areas where hybridisation and contamination are processes always *in fieri* (Franceschi, Fortunati, 2000). And it is interesting to note how much the very concept of *border* is re-evaluated today in the anthropological analysis of the contemporary world, being increasingly preferred to that of *boundary*. A border, in fact, as Ugo Fabietti explains,

> is something which separates as it unites [...] in order to imagine something which separates and unites at the same time, we must think of a kind of "no-man's land" set between two spaces (not necessarily meant to be taken in a "geographical" sense), each occupied by a society or a culture with a style different from the other (Fabietti, 1995: 104–105).

But the aspect which emerges above all in Guizot's writings is a Europe that "does not regret its lost unity" (Moretti, 1993: 840) and in which the nation states, the nation therefore, present those very characteristics identified by Renan: it is not a reality that can be objectified or described within boundaries, territorial limits or biological characteristics. In conclusion, both in the text by Guizot, and in Renan's essay, the reader is able to glimpse the spirit and the character of the imagined communities, as described by Benedict Anderson, according to whom the nation is:

> an imagined political community – and imagined as both inherently limited and sovereign. It is *imagined* because the members of even the smallest nation will never know most of their fellow-members, meet them, or even hear of them, yet in the minds of each lives the image of their communion (Anderson, 1991: 5–6).

If, therefore, the very characteristics of Europe come under the definition of Anderson's imagined community, whose "spirit is evanescent and aseptic" and whose essence is born "from the chaos, whose boundaries are uncertain, with variable geometry, susceptible to movement, to breakdown, to metamorphoses" (Morin, 1988: 29), then it is natural to question the nature of its identity, the essence of its memory. In fact, if the idea of Europe as an *unitas multiplex* was already present in the *Encyclopédie* edited by Denis Diderot (Morin, 1988: 24; Passerini, 2003: 103), it was only much later that the ideas of European specificity and identity began to be problematised; emblematic examples are the canonical stories of Europe, (Chabod, 1961; Curcio, 1958; Duroselle, 1965; Voyenne, 1964) which only touched on the question of European identity.

Speaking today of identity, and of European identity in particular, has revealed itself to be a complex operation for various reasons; one of these regards the dynamics and cultural movement of the entire planet, conditioned, if not determined, by the current delocalizations (Hannerz, 1992; Fabietti, 2000: 178) and deterritorialisations (Appadurai, 1991). From this new panorama emerges a profound dialectic between European identity and migration, whose representation, or rather "narrativisation", expresses itself and takes shape beginning from specific cultural memoirs, well-localised, but renegotiated, reconfigured and remodelled from time to time through hybridisations, half-breeds and connections (Amselle, 1990; 2001). These reflections may be able to shed light on the different concepts of *belonging* and *presence* (Fabietti, 2000), *memory* and *recollection* (Assmmann, 2002), *identity* and *identification* (Bhabha, 1990; Passerini, 2003).

Beyond biography, beyond identity

Biography and *life stories*. Analysing the two etymons may help us understand why this genre has been chosen, why this methodology has been adopted[6]. After analysing the stratified fluidity of the concept of European identity (fluidity, it should be stressed, contains the idea of *belonging* and *distance*, *identity* and *disillusionment*) we see how this stratification emerges in the actual biographical account and a spurious specificity reveals itself, an original hybridity: history and memory, recollection and oblivion play a crucial role.

In Italy, the expression *"storie di vita"* is used within the ethno-anthropological disciplines, incorporating the English terms *"life story"* and *"life history"* and obviously the French saying *"récit de vie"*. As Jacques Le Goff writes,

> in the Romance languages and others, history expresses two, if not three concepts: 1) an investigation of the actions carried out by men which has strived to construct itself in science, historical science; 2) the object of the investigation, that which men have carried out and according to Paul Veyne, history is both a succession of events and the account of this succession of events. But history may also have a third meaning, precisely that of recounting. A story is an account, which may be true or false, based on historical reality, or purely imaginary (1978: 566).

The French term *récit* expresses the idea of "reading aloud" and "narrative from memory"; the etymon of the word "biography" gives the idea of writing (*bios* and *graphia*). Various elements therefore co-exist in life stories and biographies: the desire to carry out objective research, one's own subjectivity when storytelling and "recollecting", the ability to "narrate" and even the possibility of rewriting, reconstructing. In this sense, the biography and the "life story" represent a complex methodology to define, almost "unsaid" in the history of anthropology,

---

[6] The theme of "life stories" as a literary genre or research methodology is vast. For an exhaustive treatment see Z. A. Franceschi. 2003. *Le storie di vita nelle discipline etnoantropologiche. Percorsi metodologici per una ricerca di campo* (Life stories in the ethno-anthropological disciplines. Methodological paths for field research), PhD thesis in Anthropology of Contemporaneity, XV cycle. University of Milan-Bicocca; interesting also G. Marcus 1982; A. Battistini 1990.

encompassing some of the most pressing issues of the discipline, which only modern anthropology has attempted to deal with. Always employed to gather ethnographic material, they were passed over for a long time, being human and personal "matter", the preference being to concentrate on *facts:* weddings, genealogies, customs, material culture. On these elements, the construction of objective, solid and homogeneous cultures could be founded. As regards this, it may be interesting to note how this methodology right from the beginning proved itself to be particularly suited to gather stories of immigration, in which the processes of acculturation[7] played a fundamental role in the recreation of the biographical account. The biographical fact thus became an element for demonstrating the inexistence of purity, homogeneity and cultural compactness; in fact, it is not by chance that it also became a "spokesman" for all those social and cultural stratifications such as "the culture of poverty", "the culture of illiteracy", "the culture of the Diaspora". We can try today to read "life stories" as if they were a mirror on the ethno-anthropological disciplines: their use by anthropologists accurately reflects ideologies and the influence of their thinking at a theoretical and epistemological level. They can also represent a kind of "social thermometer" which measures the levels of change and continuity, an operative thermometer that is always attentive, reminding us of the complex and intricate relationship between the individual and society. Due to their very character, unsuited to compromise and mystification, "life stories" are immediately revealed as "cultural constructions", which were not representative of the universal manner of recounting life experiences.[8] Today, the certainty that this "textualisation" has not represented the universal and natural way of recounting one's own existence clashes not only with the proliferation of autobiographies, but also with the awareness that in time they have become, in and through history, a vehicle and an instrument of the knowledge of our contemporary world, both Western and non-Western. Starting from this theoretical assumption, I have tried to develop a hypothesis that has guided – perhaps implicitly – the relationship between biography and the contemporary anthropological world. Through the meeting that takes place in a biographical narration, – a kind of an *anthropopoietic* (*anthropos*, men; *poieo*, to make) rite (Remotti, 1996 b: 9–27)[9] of initiation, – one is "reborn", changed: the "contents" of these narrations are modified and their "containers" are transformed. That which is narrated – contemporary anthropologists[10] are very clear on this point – contributes to the construction of a liminal knowledge, careful to capture the diverse and incomplete ways in which

---

[7] The autobiographies collected by P. Radin (1883–1959), anthropologist of Polish origin who worked with the Winnebago Indians, come to mind or the experience of O. Lewis (1914–1970) who collected the "life histories" of immigrants in urban environments.
[8] An interesting article by G. Gusdorf from 1956, republished with the title "Conditions and Limits of Autobiography", in J. Olney 1980.
[9] See F. Remotti 1996b.
[10] J. Clifford 1997 comes to mind.

an identity is formed. Despite its fluidity and hybridity, identity continues to preserve languages, dialects and cultures that have travelled, moved, stopped and moved on again. Biographical narration, whose anthropological equivalent is the "life story", manages to develop along very precise formal and epistemological characteristics and with certain purposes recognisable through what Amselle calls "connections" (Amselle, 2001). Life stories not only take into account the identitary stratification of everybody, but also have the ability to reshape heterogeneous cultural elements, social facts that are often discordant. Through their very value of historical and autobiographical testimony, and the fragmentary and incomplete nature which characterises them, biographical narrations and "life stories" show themselves to be a "hinge" between the "global" and the "local", the individual and society, the past, present and future of the discipline. Nowadays, in the narration, in the ways of managing the dialogue, in remaining silent or talking, in different places and using other languages, the streets, paths and tracks left by each one of us in the course of our own existence can be identified.

The testimonies capable of giving a voice to biographical paths marked by movement, by journeys, by immigration may be many.[11] Autobiographical narration assumes the shape of a "niche", a "reservoir" where an otherwise silent and perishable heritage can be kept and then "exhibited"; autobiographical writing and biographical narration, which anthropology calls "life stories", can represent the "methodology" and the "genre" that, perhaps more than others, manages to take into account the complexity of our contemporary worlds. The women, the exiled, the deported, the immigrants, the "colonised" speak, build up the narratives, re-shape the order of what is local and what is global through their stories and accounts:

> Journeying across generations and cultures, tale-telling excels in its powers of adaptation and germination; while with exile and migration, travelling expanded in time and space becomes dizzyingly complex in its repercussive effects. Both are subject to the hazards of displacement, interaction and translation. Both, however, have the potential to widen the horizon of one's imagination and to shift the frontiers of reality and fantasy, or Here and There. Both contribute to questioning the limits set on what is known as "common" and "ordinary" in daily existence, offering thereby the possibility of an elsewhere-within-here, or-there (Trinh, 1994: 11).

According to Trinh Minh-ha, the autobiographical value of recollections, memoirs and oblivion for those who have experienced "dislocation", whether voluntary or forced, is linked to a double process: that of "estrangement"[12] on the one

---

[11] The recent publication of the autobiography by E. Said 1999 comes to mind, as does the publication of biographies by less well-known figures.

[12] In literature, estrangement is a "literary technique aimed at generating a new and unusual vision of a reality which is already known, via the modification of expressive techniques and the deformation of the automatisms of everyday language. In theatre and in cinema, a sense of detachment between the spectator and the events represented,

hand and reappropriation on the other. As Trinh Minh-ha says: What they chose to recount no longer belongs to them (Trinh, 1994: 10).[13]

The material that is chosen to be deposited, "held" and then recounted, no longer belongs to he/she who remembers, nor to he/she who is remembered. It is as if the experience of otherness experienced via "estrangement" produces a spatial, temporal and identitary gap between he/she who remembers and he/she who is remembered, between he/she who sees and he/she who is seen. The result of this passage is therefore a new "product", an "imaginative investment", a "creative act". The "dislocation", the journey, the meeting with alterity encourage the creation of the biographical account, but it assumes the shape of a narration that has its own peculiarities, which distinguishes itself from the classical biography not so much in its structural paradigms as in its value and representation. Just as new wine obtained through precise fermentation techniques and bottled shortly after harvesting is particularly fragrant and sweet-smelling, this kind of biographical narration has its own manner of sedimentation during which forms change, equilibriums are transformed and configurations alter.

But let us proceed by degrees: let us begin again from identity. The category of identity, as Cristina Demaria stresses in the introduction to the essay by Stuart Hall (Hall, 2002), provocatively entitled, "Who needs identity?", "is a modern invention, which has not become problematic over the course of time, but rather was born as a problem [...], it can only exist as a problem" (Bauman, 1996 in Demaria, 2002: 119). Today, talking about identity – and above all about European identity – means starting a journey with breaks, movements, through intersecting spaces (Bhabha, 1997; Grossberg, 1996). Identities are analysed as "temporary and unstable effects of relations between differences" (Demaria, 2002: 120); talking about identity means situating oneself within specific evolutions and historical practices which have re-shaped the relatively "fixed" character of cultures and populations; exploring identity also means re-positioning oneself with respect to the process of globalisation. Finally, undertaking an analysis of the concept of identity has a meaning to the extent one has the wisdom to ask oneself not so much

> where we come from, rather what we can become, how we have been represented, and how all of this relates to our own methods of self-representation (Hall, 2002: 134).

And it is exactly in this sense that European identity should be interpreted and decoded, and it is precisely in this scenario that cultural memory acts and is constructed.

---

provoked by a director or actor by way of various techniques", see. *Vocabolario della Lingua Italiana* (Italian language dictionary), Nicola Zingarelli, twelfth edition, edited by M. Dogliotti and L. Rosiello, Zanichelli, 1996. The first theorizations on the concept of "estrangement" date back to Russian formalism. In his text, C. Ginzburg begins with a quotation by V. Šklovskij. See C. Ginzburg 1998.

[13] Our italics.

After having highlighted all the processes needed to deconstruct and dismantle the category of identity, it is impossible to deny how much identity continues to be an incessant topic of debate. Why? Which fragments has contemporaneity decided to re-use? With what potentialities? Who is witness and ambassador of European identity?

We certainly will not find exhaustive answers to these pressing questions, but the issues linked to cultural memory could supply some interesting suggestions.

Firstly, it is important to remember that recollection and oblivion are at the heart of the act of representing a nation's construction. Yet, Renan writes: "The essence of a nation lies in the very fact that all citizens have many things in common, many of which they have forgotten" (Renan, 1997: 48).

The recollection of memory, oblivion: narrating history

Cultural memory in this sense represents a legacy that each nation has created to mould its own identity. It always acts on two axes, parallel and complementary at the same time: recollection (memory) and oblivion (amnesia). If we consider the opinion of Jan Assmann, according to whom societies need the past first of all for self-definition purposes (Assman, 1992), the historical revisitation of European identity and its deconstruction "as well as expressing many political dynamics occurring in the individual national contexts, causes the cultural production of the minorities, the oppressed and the colonised to emerge, placing it in relation to the dominant culture. In such a scenario it is particularly interesting to re-read the history of European identity as a narration: "narration" in journeys, in immigration, narration that the subject represents from time to time, as articulation in the construction process of one's identity. And it is not by chance that Homi Bhabha, writing on the relationship between nation and narration (Bhabha, 1990), describes the journey and the exile that he himself experienced on the streets of different countries throughout the world:

> I have lived that moment of the scattering of the people that in other times and other places, in the nations of others, becomes a time of gathering. Gatherings of exiles and émigrés and refugees, gathering on the edge of "foreign" cultures; gathering at the frontiers; gatherings in the ghettos or cafés of city centres; gathering in the half-life, half-light of foreign tongues, or in the uncanny fluency of another's languages; gathering the signs of approval and acceptance, degrees, discourses, disciplines; gathering the memories of underdevelopment, of other worlds lived retroactively; gathering the past in a ritual of revival; gathering the present (Bhabha, 1990: 291).

Memory, recollection, and the awareness of the need for oblivion are constant and recurring themes throughout the history of contemporary anthropological literature. If we think of the historical, cultural and political reconstruction of contemporary Argentina by certain social science academics, some have spoken of "epidemics of memory", of an "excess of the past" (Lazzarato, 2003). Contrary to what is happening today, we would search in vain in the history of anthropology for specific "treatises" on memory;[14] any attempt to trace a definition of "cultural memory" would be useless. I believe the scarce attention paid to memory is linked to various factors and is extremely interesting if we think of the similar destiny to which biographies and autobiographies have been subjected throughout the history of anthropological thinking. Firstly, the study of cultural memory (because this is what anthropology should be occupying itself with) probably posed a series of epistemological problems, which anthropology in its infancy was not ready to deal with. It is not by chance that Halbwachs concentrated on collective and social memory (Halbwachs, 1925; 1968), barely touching on anything that regarded individual, personal, subjective and "emotional" memory. It may be interesting to remember the etymology of the Italian word for memory ("ricordo"): *recordāri; re-cor,* to put into the heart. In this regard, Aleida Assmann highlights Friedrich G. Jünger's precise definitions, distinguishing between the terms *Gedächtnis* (memory) and *Erinnerung* (recollection) where the former indicates the "mnestic fact" or knowledge, while the second indicates the subjective experience (Assmann, 2002: 29). In the anthropological domain therefore, the destiny of memory follows that of "life stories", biographies and autobiographies in an almost inexorable manner. It was advisable to study these as little as possible because they shed light on everything the discipline sought to conceal and to hide: the complex relationship between the anthropologist and his informer; the problems linked to the orality, transcription and translation of texts; the space-time relationship as it was lived and told by *other,* non-Western populations. Finally, talking of memory would have shed light on the complex and subtle mechanisms linking anthropology to politics and power. Franz Boas, who trained some of the most assiduous supporters of the biographical method, on biography and memory stated:

> Modern anthropological literature shows that intimate observations on individual lives are felt to be essential for further progress, and new methods have been devised to obtain the needed information. Some of these methods seem to me of doubtful value. It is obvious that, setting aside laboratory experiment, the only way to obtain the necessary information is through a most intimate and long-continued life with the people and a perfect control of their language [...] One of the methods used to overcome these difficulties is to induce natives to write or tell autobiographies. The better ones of these give us a valuable information in regard to the struggles of everyday life and of the joys and sorrows of the people, but their reliability, beyond very elementary points, is doubtful. *They are not*

---

[14] See Z. A. Franceschi: *Memory and history in the ethno-anthropological disciplines.* Essay presented in Bertinoro, May 16–18 2003 during the convention ACUME-GENERAL MEETING. See http://www.lingue.unibo.it/acume/up3.htm.

> *facts but memories and memories distorted by the wishes and thoughts of the moment* [...] Quite recently Lowie has published versions of a Crow tale, told at various time by the same individual, which show remarkable variations in plot and motives. I have published similar records of the same tale, retold by the same informant after an interval of nearly forty years, which show the stability of formal elements and the variability of motives. This is much more intensely the case in records of personal experiences. The same person has told me the incidents of his own life at one time as simple, matter-of-fact occurrences, at other times as supernatural experiences [...] *Autobiographies [...] are valuable rather as useful material for a study of the perversion of truth brought about by the play of memory with the past. The rest is not much more than an account of customs collected in the usual way* (Boas, 1942: 334-335).

Memory, autobiography and "life stories" not only represented that French "histoire événementielle" that Boasian anthropology had always treated with suspicion, but also *distorted* facts and reality, producing a kind of temporal and spatial gap between *history* and *testimony*, between *recollection* and *truth*. A second reason that led to neglecting memory was the anthropologist's controversial and ambiguous relationship with *history* and therefore with *time*. Such problems were linked to complex disciplinary relationships on the one hand and on the other to a profound discomfort with studying the representation of *other* temporalities (Fabian, 1983; Viazzo, 2000). Retracing the anthropologist's relationship with history and memory is truly complex; it is sufficient to think of the notes by Lévi-Strauss in his critique of the work of Sartre (Lévi-Strauss, 1962). Before his time, Lévi-Strauss had understood many of the issues that Geertzian and postmodern anthropology would have dealt with later, and had the following to say:

> toute recherche ethnographique a son principe dans des "confessions" écrites ou inavouées [...] Par conséquent, le fait historique n'est pas plus *donné* que les autres; c'est l'historien, ou l'agent du devenir historique, qui le constitue par abstraction, et comme sous la menace d'une régression à l'infini [...] De ce point de vue aussi, l'historien et l'agent historique choissent, tranchent et découpent, car une histoire vraiment totale les confronterait au chaos (Lévi-Strauss, 1962: 329-330-279-340).[15]

Lévi-Strauss's works are truly illuminating and still manage to be highly topical. There are very strong platonic echoes[16] in the work of the historian who selects and eliminates information and starts the process again, then puts it into boxes, orders and sifts it. Essentially, the task carried out by the historian, just like that carried out by the ethnologist, consists of a patient and detailed reconstruction,

---

[15] Italics in the text.
[16] Remotti's writings on identity construction are very interesting. See Remotti, 1996b.

in a long temporal re-adjustment, in a complicated spatial remodelling. Lévi-Strauss again:

> L'ethnologue respecte l'histoire, mais il ne lui accorde pas une valeur privilégie. Il la conçoit comme une recherche complémentaire de la sienne: l'une déploie l'éventail des sociétés humaines dans le temps, l'autre dans l'espace. Et la différence est moins grande encore qu'il ne semble, puisque l'historien s'efforce de restituer l'image des sociétés disparues telles qu'elles furent dans des instants qui, pour elles, correspondirent au présent; tandis que l'ethnographe fait de son mieux pour reconstruire les étapes historiques qui ont précédé dans le temps les formes actuelles (Lévi-Strauss, 1962: 339).

Anthropology was born with the ambition of being an "exact science", a discipline based on empirical experiments and in any case a producer of laws;[17] anthropology as an ethnographic experience, and consequently as an ethnological elaboration[18], in reality proved to be a fiction, "literary, systemic and conceptual" (Fabietti, 1999, 128–137). The very investigation of the concept of fiction (to be taken in its Latin meaning of *fingere*, to form, to mould, to create, to shape) has pushed me into reconstructing a path in which European history, immigration, memory and identity have found precarious and uncertain equilibriums, which could only be looked at from afar.

Travel and immigration: contemporary stories, old and new questions

> I was born not far from the forests because when my mother was pregnant with me ... there were all the lianas, she saw all those lianas, and that's why they called me ... they called me ... Lian.

In March 1999, I asked Lian to tell me her "life story", she agreed, and I interviewed her. Since then, we have seen each other every year, but I only allowed myself to interview her one more time. Since then, during our yearly meeting she

---

[17] The article by F. Boas, 1940 [1887], comes to mind.
[18] Here are the thoughts of Lévi-Strauss regarding ethnography and ethnology: "Restent à définir l'ethnographie elle-même, et l'ethnologie. Nous les distinguerons, de façon très sommaire et provisoire, mais suffisante au début de l'enquête, en disant que l'ethnographie consiste dans l'observation et l'analyse de groupes humains considérés dans leur particularité (souvent choisis, pour des raisons théoriques et pratiques, mais qui ne tiennent nullement à la nature de la recherche, armi ceux qui diffèrent le plus de nôtre), et visant à la restitution, aussi fidèle que possible, de la vie de chacun d'eux ; tandis que l'ethnologie utilise de façon comparative (et à des fins qu'il faudra déterminer par la suite) les documents présentés par l'ethnograhe.", in: Lévi-Strauss 1958, 4–5. This article appeared in 1949 with the title "Histoire et Ethnologie". In: *Revue de Métaphisique et Morale*, LVI, n. 3-4, pp. 363–391.

has told me her life story: as she wanted, in the ways she preferred, always in the same place. Here I will attempt to reconstruct this "life", to put this "story" down on paper, just as I heard it told, beginning from March 1999. Already on that day in March, I understood from Lian that she was not willing to open up her entire existence to me. She informed me through precise signals and above all with her affable, stubborn and determined way of storytelling, that only certain episodes would be recounted in detail; this was a part of her life that she wanted to reconstruct. In the biographical account reconstructed by me, a decision was made to use two names: Liane (the actual name of my interlocutor) and Juliette, a kind of "pseudonym" used to highlight the degree to which "story" and "history" merge and interweave in the ethnographic reconstruction of a biography, finding unexpected ways to reconstruct and remould themselves. The life of my interlocutor, just as it was reconstructed over years of field research, can be described as follows.

Liane Perotti was born in Bien Hoa on November 21, 1909, the oldest of four sisters. Her mother, a Vietnamese woman named Le Thi-Khoung, gave birth to other three girls. Her father Bonifacio immigrated to Indochina in 1908. Bonifacio was a cooper, just like his father before him. Juliette lived in Cambodia and Indochina until she was 13. Her father became a public works contractor for the French government, mainly designing and building bridges. He was continually moving from place to place and so decided to send his three remaining daughters – Juliette herself, Giuseppina and Mary – to study in Italy (the family originally came from Piedmont). The three sisters spent their childhood and part of their adolescence in boarding school, in Virle. Juliette married as soon as she finished her studies in 1930, while Giuseppina returned to stay with her father who was in Saigon at the time. Left alone, the youngest, Mary, fell ill and died of tuberculosis. Juliette too returned to her father in Indochina as soon as she could. Between the beginning of the first Resistance and the French withdrawal from Indochina (1945–1954), the Perotti family returned to Europe: Bonifacio and Giuseppina were "naturalised" as French citizens and settled in Paris; Juliette, her husband and their children returned to Italy and went to stay in Bologna where her husband's family originated from. Juliette never left Italy again and Giuseppina settled in Paris with her husband and children in the same way.

The "fieldwork" with Juliette began with a first interview in March 1999. Later, we spent 15 days together in 1999, 2000 and 2001 in the family home in Piedmont. Various documents and family photographs, which have been catalogued and reorganised, were found during this stay. On these occasions, Juliette was always willing to retell and remember her past. Given the impossibility of reconstructing Lian's entire "life story", I feel it is appropriate to investigate my reasons not only for using a false name, Juliette, but also for often maintaining her real given name. Lian recounted a part of her life to me and decided to select certain precise episodes.[19] Observing the methods of reconstructing this biography (adopted by Lian and myself), I realised while Lian was talking, selecting events and occurrences, choosing words and images, that it was necessary to adopt a second name: Juliette. Such a strategy could take into account certain methodological needs implied by the narration. Lian's name, maintained over the course of the entire research will seek to show the difficult process of mediation carried out by this woman for what she *chose* to represent during each of our meetings. There was the account, the "representation" of her existence, its reconstruction, and. at the same time, there was a historical identity that was represented by the documents and photographs and thus linked to her entire biographical path, to her "story". Therefore, the use of the two names, Lian and Juliette, intends to show the difficult balance between history and retelling, between the "oral biography" (Clemente, 1982; 1988) and the anthropological life story (Callari, Galli, 1966).

Lian and Juliette, Juliette and Lian: each brings a story, an account, a different life. Before beginning the reconstruction of Juliette's "life story", I believe it may be interesting to understand what happened on that day in March 1999, when Lian decided to narrate her biography to me, when Juliette's "life story" slowly took shape. On that day that Lian made a decision that she no longer wanted to turn back from: I would get to know the life of Juliette, she would recount that part of her existence to me, I would become the one who listened, who patiently transcribed her every word; but above all I was the one who would accept that tacit agreement. Lian did not even want to acknowledge the existence of this long path through memories, recollections, photographs and old stories.

The use of a pseudonym capable of preserving the intimacy of she who has recounted her life to me over the course of these last three years eliminates perhaps the only "fixed point in a moving world" (Ziff, in Bourdieu, 1995: 74), the only official testimonial to a "constant and lasting social identity": one's given first name. I have not heard recounted, nor have I re-written the story of Lian, but I was permitted to listen to and "record" certain events of Juliette's life. What implications can this "passage" have, this "metamorphosis" which fills each moment of the narration, in the operations of reconstructing and "re-stitching" a life, in the practice of getting to know and interpreting a "story"? And what consequences will this "appellative alteration", and therefore identitary alteration, carry into the concrete path of the life of Lian? And into that of Juliette? According to Pierre Bourdieu,

> En tant qu'institution, le nom propre est arraché au temps et à l'espace, et aux variations selon les lieux et les moments: par là, il assure aux individus désigné, par delà tous les changements et toutes les fluctuations biologiques et sociales, la *constance nominale*, l'identité au sens d'identité à soi-même, de *constantia sibi,* que demande l'ordre social [...] Le nom

---

[19] It is in this sense that an attempt will be made to reconstruct the "account" of a life, "le récit de vie", "the life story".

> propre est l'attestation visible de l'identité de son porteur à travers les temps et les espaces sociaux, le fondement de l'unité de ses manifestations successives et de la possibilité socialement reconnue de totaliser ces manifestations dans des enregistrements officiels *curriculum vitae, cursus honorum,* casier judiciaire, nécrologie ou biographie qui constituent la vie en totalité finie par le verdict porté sur un bilan provisoire ou définitif (Bourdieu, 1986: 70).

The continuity and coherence with ourselves, with one's own individual path, in the opinion of Bourdieu, is ensured through the attribution of one's first name, at least in its most "external" implications. In this regard, Bourdieu does not reveal to us what, in his opinion, biography represents, neither as a "literary genre", much less as an "exploratory methodology". He only tells us what it should not represent: a "story". Bourdieu is very careful not to enter into the discussion of the various meanings that this term can have: investigation, account, object of investigation. The "life story" remains an "illusion": Dont la constance n'est sans doute que celle d'un nom propre (Bourdieu, 1986: 71).

Clearly, the use of a pseudonym also eliminates that sole constant (one's first name) found by Bourdieu. In using a pseudonym, the anthropological "life story" sets the first rule of the ethics of a silent and memorable pact with the reader, academy and society, and, according to the interpretation of Pierre Bourdieu, can neither be considered an "artificiality" or an "illusion". It will cease to exist even as a trajectory, route or passage, being discontinued, ephemeral and evanescent in any case. A different position, more stimulating in this context, seems to be the one held by Philippe Lejeune:

> Les pseudonymes littéraires ne sont en général ni des mystères, ni des mystifications; le second nom est aussi authentique que le premier, il signale simplement cette second naissance qu'est l'écriture publiée. Écrivant son autobiographie, l'auteur à pseudonyme en donnera lui-même l'origine: ainsi, Raymond Abellio explique qu'il s'appelle Georges Soulès, et pourquoi a choisi son pseudonyme. Le pseudonyme est simplement une différenciation, in dédoublement du nom, qui ne change rien à l'identité (Lejeune, 1975: 24).[20]

According to Philippe Lejeune, pseudonyms therefore indicate the existence of a second life, which, it should be stressed, is found in the text and in the published text. On paper, through the act of writing, it is as if the subject were born for a second time; the autobiography, as already noted by Gusdorf in 1975, represents a veritable "rite of initiation". However, in this "second life" nothing changes in terms of form or content in the identity of the work and the author in question, because we must not forget that autobiography, as interpreted by Lejeune in *Le*

---

[20] Our italics.

Pacte Autobiographique, "ne comporte pas de degrés: c'est tout ou rien" (Lejeune, 1975: 25).

Another matter is the autobiographical novel; here the use of the pseudonym could lead to changes, to similarities in the identity between author and protagonist and in whatever else was desired. The autobiographical novel, as opposed to the autobiography, "admits degrees" (Lejeune, 1986: 25). "Degrees", we will see, are also admitted in the "life story", in the anthropological biography. Here, too, it is as if retelling, just like the writing of one's own biographical path, assumes a kind of "rite of passage", a "rite of initiation" a new life (Van Gennep, 1981). Which identity could transform itself? That of the reader? That of he who has recounted his own existence? Because, if we think about it carefully from an anthropological point of view, the attribution of a second name acquires the features of a ritual and we must not forget that the purpose of any ritual, of whatever nature or in whatever context it is represented, is to bring about profound changes in the human being's social and individual status. In reality, Bourdieu had already set us on the right track because, despite having dismissed the biography as a mere ideological construction, he had connected the "first name" to the social ritual belonging to it.[21] The attribution of the "first name", that of a new name, and that of a pseudonym therefore, represent a highly respected ritual moment. Biographies and "life stories" as an anthropological methodology (as opposed to the autobiography) systematically using the pseudonym show themselves to contain a veritable "ritual performance".[22] The need to use a pseudonym together with the original first name, once more stresses not only the identitary stratification, but also the recourse to the notion of *pretence* in the complex reconstruction of an account, of a story, of *one* belonging.

Having listened to the story of Juliette as narrated by her, together with the story of her father Bonifacio, and having understood to which degree the ritual is an issue linked to a process of remodelling and readjustment, I tried to follow a path that allowed me to find a common thread linking interviews, informal dialogues, family documents, and literary and historical sources. Many times I have wondered about the meaning of this narration; the anthropological value of a story so complex to reconstruct. In the interviews, Juliette formally narrated that part of her life linked to her own and her father's experience in Indochina, while recounting her life in Piedmont and all of those more personal and autobiographical details of Indochina, the anecdotes, the "trifles" in a more informal manner (free conversation, informal discussions, "chats"). She did not speak of certain years or many people who had affected her existence. She did this to preserve an experience of pain and suffering, but also to "give" me that part of her life that

---

[21] P. Bourdieu does not make a real distinction between biography and life story. Perhaps because in any case, as we have previously stressed, in French, *récit* does not distinguish between *story* and *history* as English does.

[22] In anthropological research the use of a pseudonym, or simply the initials, establishes a kind of "silent pact" between the researcher, his interlocutors and the scientific academy.

she considered interesting for me, for my research, for my studies. Juliette wanted to give me the "gift" of a piece of *history*[23]. Examining the material closely and looking at this story from afar, "longitudinally" and over time, has led me to develop an epistemological paradigm focused on identity construction: over these years, in each of her narrations, this woman has tried to reconstruct her identity as a woman and as an immigrant woman who has travelled throughout her entire existence, learning languages and dialects and growing in different cultural and social environments.

Over these years of research, the "formative process" that this woman has adopted during each of her accounts has emerged during each phase of narration. The procedures of identitary construction have in fact highlighted a complex identity; the will and the desire to put in order and reconstruct one's own life clash in each narration with a mixed identity, multiple rather than two-fold. Liane and Juliette have demonstrated the value not only of memory and recollection but also and inexorably the need for oblivion (Ricoeur, 2000).

Conclusions

Identitary processes are therefore metabolic processes of transformation and alteration. In remembering, Juliette "cuts and sews", "knots back together and separates". But that which may be interesting to observe is, *what does it begin from*? Or rather, *what separates from what*? Answering these questions is a complex matter. Following the advice of James Clifford (1997), it makes more sense today to ask ourselves, "which places has she moved between?" This woman has travelled, she has migrated, she has put down roots many times and left again just as often. And what has she brought with her? How and where has she been able to preserve her "Piedmontesity"? It is very difficult to circumscribe her belonging, complex and stratified as it is. Juliette's places may be thought of as borders, areas of contamination, but also of vigilance and affirmation. Juliette would surely place herself on a line of fracture. Following Amselle's line of thinking, or similarly, that of Bhabha, it may be interesting to ask ourselves the following; if it is true that the binary and dichotomous distinctions have collapsed, and that those which emerge today are the "in-between" zones, the interstices (where the processes of contamination and hybridisation are prevalent), can we then rethink the "rules" that control the process of connection and disconnection? And in what way? If, as Edgar Morin has suggested, a "reform of think-

---

[23] C. Jourdan has the following to say regarding the double register used by his interlocutor Resina: "But Resina did not simply recount her life. Staying within the limits of veracity and sometimes, out of the bounds of her own consciousness, Resina projected visions of her life, for herself, as much as for me. In some respects, she told the story that she wanted to tell. In others, she told the story that she thought I wanted to hear. In many instances, she became carried away by the story itself, enthralled in the drama that she was describing, fusing fact and fiction" (Jourdan, 1997: 48–49).

ing" is necessary, it is certain that today there are different, incomplete and provisional ways in which both the *identitary belonging* and the *journey* are realised. The example of the life story I have gathered and presented here may be observed and read in relation to the complexity of the contemporary worlds through an in-depth rethinking of the concept of European identity. How do processes that assail the macrostructures (Diasporas, exiles, means of communication) touch the daily lives of those who have already lived and who are still living on boundary lines? This cultural fluidity that places the accent on original syncretism, in which one seeks to avoid taxonomic classifications and any "metaphysics of sedentariness" (Callari Galli, 2000; Callari Galli, Ceruti, Pievani, 1998; Amselle, 1990), where does it set the individual, his historical and social memory, if it is a "half-breed memory" on one hand, is it a very precise and well "localised" historical memory on the other?

References

AMSELLE, J. L. 1990: Logiques métisses. Anthropologie de l'identité en Afrique et ailleurs. Paris: Payot.
AMSELLE, J. L. 2001: Branchements. Anthropologie de l'universalitè des cultures. Paris: Flammarion.
ANDERSON, B. 1991: Imagined Communities. London-New York: Verso.
APPADURAI, A. 1991: Global Ethnoscapes: Notes and Queries for a Transitional Anthropology. In: R. G. Fox (ed.), Recapturing Anthropology. Working in the Present. Santa Fe, N.M.: School of American Research Press.
APPADURAI, A. 1996: Modernity at Large: Cultural Dimension of Globalization. Minneapolis: University of Minnesota Press.
ASSMANN, J. 1992: Das kulturelle Gedächtnis. Schrift, Erinnerung und politische Identität in frühen Hochkulturen. München: Beck'sche Verlagsbuchhandlung.
ASSMANN, A. 2002: Erinnerungsräume. Formen und Wandlungen des kulturellen Gedächtnissen. München: C. H. Beck'sche Verlagsbuchhandlung.
BATTISTINI, A. 1990: Lo specchio di Dedalo, autobiografia e biografia. Bologna: Il Mulino.
BHABHA, H. K. 1990: The Third Space. In: J. Rutherford (ed.), Identity, Community, Culture, Difference. London: Lawrence & Wishart.
BHABHA, H. K. (ed.) 1990: Nation and Narration. London: Routledge.
BOAS, F. 1943: Recent Anthropology. In: Science, Vol. 8, pp. 311–337 [Read before the American Ethnological Society, May 13, 1942].
BIANCHI C., DEMARIA C., NERGAARD A. 2002: Spettri del potere. Ideologia identità traduzione negli studi culturali. Roma: Meltemi.
BOAS, F. 1940 [1887]: The Study of Geography. In: Race, Language and Culture. New York: McMillan.
BOURDIEU, P. 1986: L'illusion biographique. In: Actes de la recherche en Sciences sociales, n. 62–63, pp. 69–72.

BRAIDOTTI, R. 1994: Nomadic Subjects: Embodiment and Sexual Difference in Contemporary Feminist Theory. New York: Columbia University Press.
CALLARI GALLI, M. 1966: Le storie di vita nelle analisi culturali di Robert Redfield, Oscar Lewis, Cora DuBois. Roma: Edizioni Ricerche.
CALLARI GALLI, M. 1996: Lo spazio dell'incontro. Roma: Meltemi.
CALLARI GALLI, M., CERUTI, M., PIEVANI, T. 1998: Pensare la diversità. Per un'educazione alla complessità umana. Roma: Meltemi.
CHABOD, F. 1961: Storia dell'idea di Europa. Bari: Laterza.
CLEMENTE, P. 1988: Autobiografie al magnetofono. Una introduzione. In: V. Di Piazza, D. Mugnaini, Io so' nata a Santa Lucia. Firenze: Società Storica della Valdelsa, pp. 7–20.
CLEMENTE, P. 1982: Per l'edizione critica di testi biografici orali. Appunti. In: Fonti Orali. Studi e Ricerche. Istituto Piemontese di Scienze economiche e sociali "Antonio Gramsci", pp.63–69.
CLIFFORD, J., MARCUS, G. E. 1986: Writing Culture. The Poetics and Politics of Ethnography. Berkeley: University of California Press.
CLIFFORD, J. 1997: Routes. Travel and Translation in the Late Twentieth Century. Cambridge (MA): Harvard University Press.
CURCIO, C. 1958: Europa. Storia di un'idea. Firenze: Vallecchi.
DEMARIA, C. 2002: Figure e strategie dell'identità postcoloniale. In: C. Bianchi, C. Demaria, A. Nergaard, Spettri del potere. Ideologia identità traduzione negli studi culturali. Roma: Meltemi, pp. 119–129.
DERIDDA, J. 1991: L'altro capo. La democrazia aggiornata. Milano: Garzanti.
DUROSELLE, J. B. 1965 [1964]: L'Idée d'Europe dans l'histoire. Paris: Denoel.
FABIAN, J. 1983: Time and Other. New York: Columbia University Press.
FABIETTI, U. 1995: L'identità etnica. Storia e critica di un concetto equivoco. Roma: La Nuova Italia Scientifica.
FABIETTI, U. 1999: Antropologia Culturale. L'esperienza e l'interpretazione. Roma-Bari: Laterza.
FABIETTI, U., MALIGHETTI, R., MATERA, V. 2000: Dal tribale al globale. Introduzione all'antropologia. Milano: Mondadori.
FONTANA, J. 1995 [1994]: L'Europa allo specchio. Storia di un'identità distorta. Roma-Bari: Laterza.
FORTUNATI, V., FRANCESCHI, Z. A. 2000: Nazione e Utopia: Elementi comuni nella costruzione di due concetti ambivalenti. In: Nell'anno 2000. Dall' Utopia all'Ucronia. Firenze: Leo S. Olschki Editore.
FORTUNATI, V. 1996: Il concetto di Europa nel Romanticismo. In: La Questione Romantica. Napoli: Liguori, pp. 15–23.
FRANCESCHI, Z. A. 2002: Le storie di vita nelle discipline etno-antropologiche. Percorsi metodologici per una ricerca di campo. Tesi di dottorato in Antropologia della contemporaneità XV ciclo. Università di Milano-Bicocca.
FRANCESCHI, Z. A. 2002: La vecchiaia tra memoria sociale e memoria autobiografica: un percorso interdisciplinare. Resoconto di una ricerca di campo.

In: Guerci, S. Consigliere (cura di), La vecchiaia nel tempo. Genova: Erga Edizioni, pp.339–352.

GADAMER, H. G. 1987: La molteplicità d'Europa. Eredità e futuro. In: A. Krali (cura di), L'identità Culturale Europea tra germanesimo e latinità. Milano: Jaca Book.

GINZBURG, C. 1998: Straniamento. Preistoria di un procedimento letterario. In: Occhiacci di legno. Nove riflessioni sulla distanza. Milano: Feltrinelli.

GUIZOT, M. 1871: Histoire de la civilization en Europe. Paris: Librairie Académique.

GUSDORF, G. 1980 [1956]: Conditions and Limits of Autobiography. In: J. Olney (ed.), Autobiography: Essays Theoretical and Critical. Princeton: Princeton University Press.

GROSSBERG, L. 1996: Identity and Cultural Studies: Is that All There Is. In: S. Hall, P. Du Gay (ed.), Question of Cultural Identity. London-Thousand Oaks-New Delhy: Sage.

HALL, S. 2002 [1996]: A chi serve l'identità? In: C. Bianchi, C. Demaria, A. Nergaard (cura di), Spettri del potere. Ideologia identità traduzione negli studi culturali. Roma: Meltemi, pp. 129–155.

HALBWACHS, M. 1968 [1950]: La mémoire collective. Paris: Presses Universitaires de France.

HALBWACHS, M. 1925: Les cadres sociaux de la mémoire. Paris: PUF.

HANNERZ, U. 1992: Cultural Complexity: Studies in the Social Organization of Meaning. New York: Columbia University Press.

HIRSCHMANN, U. 1993: Noi senzapatria. Bologna: Il Mulino.

HOBSBAWM, E. J., RANGER T. 1992 [1983]: The Invention of Tradition. Cambridge: Cambridge University Press.

JAMIN, J. 1980: Un sacré collège ou les apprentis sorciers de la sociologie. In: Cahiers internationaux de sociologie, n. 68.

JOURDAN, C. 1997: Resina's Life Histories. In: Canberra Anthropology, vol. 20, no. 1-2, pp. 40–54.

LAZZARATO, F. 2003: Volti e ricordi per il futuro. Il Manifesto. 14 agosto 2003.

LE GOFF, J. 1978: Storia. In: Enciclopedia. Torino: Einaudi, pp. 566–671.

LEJEUNE, P. 1975: Le pacte autobiographique. Paris, Editions du Seuil.

LÉVI-STRAUSS, C. 1958: Anthropologie Structurale. Paris: Plon.

LÉVI-STRAUSS, C. 1962: La Pensée Sauvage. Paris: Plon.

MARCUS, G. 1982: Rhetoric and Ethnographic Genre in Anthropological Research. In: J. Ruby (ed.), A Crack in the Mirror. Reflexive Perspectives in Anthropology. Philadelphia: University of Pennsylvania Press.

MORETTI, F. 1993: La letteratura Europea. In: P. Anderson, M. Aymard, Q. Bairoch, W. Barberis, C. Ginzburg, Storia d'Europa, vol. 1. Torino: Einaudi, 837–866.

MORIN, E. 1988: Pensare l'Europa. Milano: Feltrinelli.

Novalis, 1995 [1799]: La Cristianità o Europa. A. Reale (cura di). Milano: Rusconi.

OLNEY, J. 1980: Autobiography: Essays Theoretical and Critical. Princeton, Princeton University Press.
PASSERINI, L. (cura di) 1998: Identità Culturale Europea. Idee, Sentimenti, Relazioni. Firenze: La Nuova Italia.
PASSERINI, L. 2003: Memoria e Utopia. Il primato dell'intersoggettività. Torino: Bollati Boringhieri.
POUTIGNAT, P., STREIFF-FENART, J. 1995: Théories de l'ethnicité. Paris: PUF.
REMOTTI, F. 1996 a: Contro l'identità. Roma-Bari: Laterza.
REMOTTI, F. 1996 b: Tesi per una prospettiva antropo-poietica. In: S. Allovio, A. Favole (cura di), Le Fucine Rituali. Temi di antropo-poiesi. Torino: Il Segnalibro.
RENAN, E. 1997 [1947–61]: Cos'è una nazione. In: H. K. Bhabha (cura di), Nazione e Narrazione. Meltemi: Roma, pp. 43–63.
RICOEUR, P. 2000: La Mémoire, l'Histoire, L'Oubli. Paris: Seuil.
SAID, E. W. 1999: Out of place: a memoir. London: Granta Books.
TRINH, M. T. 1994: Other than Myself/My Other Self. In: G. Robertson, M. Mash, L. Tickner, J. Bird, B. Curtis, T. Putnam (ed.), Travellers' Tales. Narratives of Home and Displacement. London and New York: Routledge.
VAN GENNEP, A. 1981 [1909]: I Riti di Passaggio. Torino: Bollati Boringhieri.
VIAZZO, P. 2000: Introduzione all'antropologia storica. Roma-Bari: Laterza.
VOYENNE, B. 1964: Histoire de l'idée européenne. Paris: Payot.

Transnational Migrations: the Decline of the Nation-State?

Anthropological Reflections

Bruno Riccio

Introduction

In January 1999, the Nobel Laureate in economics Amartya Sen, on his way to the renowned conference of the World Economic Forum that is held yearly in Davos in Switzerland, was stopped at the frontier because he was without visa. The Swiss Police did not find the explanations provided in this regard satisfactory; the conference organizers had promised him that the visa would have been delivered at the airport. Other kinds of guarantee, for example his credit card and his US residency permit, were not useful. His Indian passport was not equivalent to an American one, or to that of one of the European member states! With this anecdote, the anthropologist Trouillot (2001) begins his recent theoretical reflections on the relevance of the anthropology of the state in an age of globalisation. The contribution presented here is located within this debate. I would like to argue against the widespread assumption within the anthropology of contemporary worlds according to which the development of transnational social networks of migratory groups necessarily erodes the relevance of the nation state in social and cultural life. At the beginning of the 1990s, a new theoretical and methodological approach to migration developed focusing on migrants' ability to sustain multi-stranded social relations that link their societies of origin and settlement. In this way, they formed transnational networks that cross cultural, geographic, and political borders. As with other dimensions of globalisation, transnational migration is often considered a social phenomenon that defies the territorial sovereignty and power of nation states over collective identities. Consequently, in the age of transnationalism and globalisation it seems obsolete to carry on the research process that could be defined as the "anthropology of the state" (cf. Grillo, 1980).

The aim of this discussion is therefore twofold. First, I illustrate theoretically as well as ethnographically the relevance of the state in affecting transnational social formations. Furthermore, I argue in favour of a transnational approach that flirts with – instead of avoiding – the ethnography of organisational, institutional and state-like practices.

With this purpose in mind, I will provide an introduction to recent attempts to shape a transnational anthropology and to some examples of the ethnography of transnationality. Then, I will refer to the Senegalese experience to show how access to power in the states of origin may imply numerous activities aimed at gaining migrants' potential economic and political resources and how the states of immigration are able to affect the life of transnational migrants. On the other side of the spectrum, by taking into account the multiple world of social policies towards migrants, I will show how Senegalese transnational strategies are however bound to be negotiated with social practitioners who favour migrants' sedentarisation. Scott (1998) argues that a perennial project of the state is that of settling people within a defined territory. Thus, the state has always been an enemy of people on the move. It is interesting, in this regard, to appreciate how this disposition persists with the discourses that animate migration policies, despite the transformation of local and national state apparatuses. I will conclude with an invitation to avoid an over-reified conception of the state in favour of an ethnography that encompasses the interplay between transnational networks and the diverse institutional practices within the various organisational cultures that shape a receiving context. I think that this methodological approach helps represent the different perspectives that characterise the migratory phenomenon and thus help strengthen the anthropology of migration.

The anthropology of migration and the ethnography of transnationality

The recent anthropology of migration has undergone major theoretical and methodological transformations, profiting from the highlight on emerging anti-essentialism: this has happened due to diverse efforts aimed at creating a transnational anthropology capable of analysing the increasingly complex "contemporary worlds" (Callari Galli, 2003; Rossi, 2003). Gradually taking a step back from strongly localised traditional studies, contemporary trends are more willing to explore the sphere of the imagination, to see the diaspora as a condition of living with its emerging plural identities, as well as the imagined construction of localities and of the diverse cultural flows of the global era, migration being one among other aspects (Appadurai, 1996; Clifford, 1997). Migrants thus become a symbol of hybridity or creolisation (Hannerz 1996) and of various forms of liberating and transgressive articulations of the relationship between locations, cultures and identities, which can no longer be conceived as natural and static (Gupta, Ferguson, 1997).

Some authors claim that the abstract and celebratory tone of transnational anthropology is premature, accusing it of exalting a model of marginal people and not taking into sufficient account their effective marginalisation (Amit-Talai 1998). Nonetheless, there are differences among the various "transnational approaches" to migration (Vertovec, 1999). For instance, transnational ethnography considers transnationalism more as a social morphology (web, community, movement or social field) and, through its "multi-sited" ethnographic enquiries, focuses specifically on migration and the study of concrete social relationships.

Indeed, many scholars and observers have highlighted the multiple ways through which some migrants remain oriented towards return, maintaining a strong identification with their sending context. Trying to overcome the "bipolar" model that tended to represent the migrant as one "uprooted" from a context considered as unchangeable, someone who tries hard to "integrate" within a different context (also considered as monolithic), ethnographies of contemporary migration have tried to call attention to the ability developed by many migrants to be part of both contexts at once. In his pioneering, Roger Rouse (1991) illustrating the "transnational migration circuit" that connects the mobile sending and receiving contexts of Mexico and the US where people, things and information flow, shows how experiences and identifications can be shared within such a circuit. Relationships and the most intimate links can be maintained even at a long distance and the tensions and social contradictions within one site can easily be reversed within the other.

Some anthropologists have defined "transnationalism" as the process through which migrants, using technological innovations, are capable of creating and maintaining social, economic, cultural and political relations, which, by connecting their sending and receiving societies, cross national borders (Glick Schiller et al., 1992). This approach, moreover, is characterised by its capacity to highlight the "micro" dimension often missing in many analyses of globalisation: multi-local ethnographies are focused therefore on the experiences of people in daily life. The flood of objects and ideas is thus considered an integral part of the social relations that migrants meet as active subjects of transnational social fields. The transnational approach constitutes an important innovation, if compared to the theories focused mainly on receiving contexts, since it allows us to take into account the socio-cultural background of migrants and their links within the sending context more accurately and systematically.

The application of a transnational approach can also be very useful to adequately understand the receiving contexts themselves. Some migrants can deal with the numerous difficulties resulting from the transformation of a world-capitalism, which is increasingly turning to liberalisation, by addressing themselves both to their sending and receiving contexts in order to create new, transnational life-strategies. As with the Congo traders based in France, studied by MacGaffey and Bazenguissa-Ganga (2000), for other migrants, too, their transnational networks can be a resource to "resist exclusion" in their homelands and abroad. Yet, some authors have expressed some perplexity about the novelty of transnationalism and of a transnational approach alike to migration (Amit-Talai, 1998; Grillo, 2000). Indeed, the premise that multiple networks connect several contexts in a continuous manner has been previously illustrated in some work of British anthropology of the colonial and post-colonial era (Epstein, 1958; Parkin, 1969; Grillo, 1973). These studies were already dealing with the circularity that binds together the rural and the urban contexts through social networks. On the other hand, others have pointed out that, for a number of reasons including globalisation, technological innovations and decolonisation processes, transnational networks are able to work to a previously unknown intensity: to a global extent and almost in real time (Smith and Guarnizo, 1998). Therefore, speed, intensity and frequency are the new characters of contemporary transnationalism. Basch Glick Schiller and Szanton-Blanc provide the following premises for a theoretical scheme for a transnational approach (1994: 22):

- a) "Transnational migration is inextricably linked to the changing conditions of global capitalism and must be analysed within the context of global relations between capital and labour.
- b) Transnationalism is a process by which migrants, through their daily activities and social, economic, and political relations, create social fields that cross national boundaries.
- c) Bounded social science concepts that conflate physical location, culture, and identity can limit the ability of researchers first to perceive and then to analyze the phenomenon of transnationalism.
- d) By living their lives across borders, transmigrants find themselves confronted with and engaged in the nation-building processes of two or more nation-states. Their identities and practices are configured by hegemonic categories, such as race and ethnicity, that are deeply embedded in the nation-building processes of these nation-states."

Although I share the focus on actors, their everyday experiences and social relations, and the critique of bounded concepts of culture and identity, I nevertheless find the other theoretical assumptions (a and c) more interesting as subjects of investigation rather than as premises from which to start research. For instance, the influences of and the resistances to "global capitalism" are not the same in every context. Furthermore, although some transnational practices may be revealed to be crucial to nation-building processes – as in the case of long distance nationalism (Anderson, 2001) – this characteristic does not emerge in many other cases of transnational formations. For this reason the less political and more generic term of "transnationality" has here been preferred to "trans-nationalism" (see Ong, 1999). It is important to highlight the contextual relevance of a whole number of factors that are able to influence transnational migration. For instance, the different degrees of inclusion and exclusion, the access of migrants to the public, social and political sphere, their legal and economic situation, both in their homelands and in the receiving countries, all constitute crucial aspects in determining diverse transnational strategies.

Such reflections lead to the relationship between transnational migration and the state. Within both of the above-mentioned streams, "transnational anthropology" and the most migration-oriented "ethnography of transnationality", there are authors who see transnational migration as a symptom of the decline of the nation state. Kearney (1996), observing how due to migration the Mixtec community, once rural, has become transnational because it is able to constantly penetrate the borders between Mexico and the United States, suggests that we are in a "post-national" era where communities erode the control of the states, transcending their defining power to fix categories of identity for individuals. As for the joint effects of electronic mass mediatisation and of transnational migration, Appadurai affirms in a more assertive manner that the state as a complex political modern formation, as well as the epoch of the nation state, have reached a "terminal crisis":

> "In a world of people on the move, of global commoditazation and states incapable of delivering basic rights even to the majority ethnic populations, territorial sovereignty is an increasingly difficult justification for those nation-states that are increasingly dependent on foreign labor, expertise, arms, or soldiers" (1996: 39).

Both Kearney and Appadurai stress the counter-hegemonic nature of transnational practices and illustrate them as acts of resistance to the definitory and regulatory power of nation states. Although I understand the reasons underlying these positions, I nevertheless believe that they risk confusing the potentialities with the realities of daily social life. First, the state is obviously important for transnationalism, since it is located in its own definition: transmigrants are those whose daily lives are "here" and "there", between two or more nation states, with profound consequences both for migrants and for the states they pass through. Furthermore, the states' power of exclusion and disciplinary strength are still very active and the state in some cases can act as a creative actor in the economic or political use of transnational networks. Robert Smith, for instance (1998), underlines the active role of the Mexican state in the use and organisation of the transnational community in the receiving context (New York). More precisely, he illustrates the historical path by which the community of migrants coming from Tijuana has benefited from being repeatedly involved in projects of the local and then the national authorities. Besides the development micro-projects and the institutionalisation of electoral mechanisms, aimed at facilitating distance voting, such activities became more concrete in the nineties with the growth of a multiplicity of recreational associations, which proved to be the organisational actors most capable of maintaining transnational relations.

Other authors affirm that in different parts of the world, as different from one another as Asia, the United States and Europe, nation states, far from losing their sovereignty and power, are now adapting and redefining their practices to manage the consequences of global economic restructuring (Ong, 1999). In Europe, especially with regard to migration policies, nation states still maintain absolute sovereignty over decision-making and whilst globalisation entails the diminishing power of nation states in some domains, they retain powerful regulatory capacity in areas that are crucial for the functioning of the new capitalist organisation. Within western capitalist economies, states are adapting their roles to the changing economic contingencies by cutting public expenditure and restructuring or even dismantling welfare systems, and concurrently controlling migration flows (Gledhill, 1998). The development of transnational networks could thus serve to further stimulate the transformation of the nation state as we are used to conceiving it, rather than totally losing its functions, especially those of control and policing. Our reflection will now focus on a specific case of transnational migration that highlights the relevance of both the sending and receiving states.

The Senegalese in Italy as an example of transnationality

Senegalese migration to Italy represents a good example of transnational migration. When Senegalese migrants talk about it they do not necessarily use the most fashionable term in contemporary migration studies, but explicitly affirm: "living part of the year in Italy and part in Senegal, you seek to exploit the two countries as best as possible". Contemporary Senegal is characterised by a precarious economic and social situation, as well as by a fragile balance between *cleavages* that historically have tended to cross each other in order to mitigate the potential conflicts that could have emerged. Since the 60s, the population has more than doubled: from 3 to 7 million inhabitants with a striking number of young people in the population, which has consequences on the increase of dependent family members (see Diop, 2002). Many young Senegalese think they do not have any other choice than to leave *(dem)* since the partial reduction of governmental funding to the agricultural sector, high prices and prohibitive taxation make earning a subsistence level income in the countryside ever more difficult. Temporary returns by migrants, especially when characterised by a degree of ostentation of their accumulated wealth, influence the imagination of the people who remain, and as such also create a symbolic incentive for departure as well as a culture of emigration (Riccio, 2000).

Senegalese transnationality means they engage in economic transactions (including trade) across international boundaries, and over a considerable distance, spending much of their time away from their place of origin, but returning there at fairly frequent intervals with the overall goal of creating an economic, social and spiritual life for themselves and their families in Senegal. This orientation towards return instead of settlement is another factor that characterises Senegalese migratory experiences (Riccio, 2002). Many emigrate mainly for economic reasons and in particular because of the crisis of the traditional agricultural system. There are about 35 000 Senegalese in Italy migrating as individuals, following social networks and connections. The fact that they are mainly men (94%) testifies to their identification with a male and mobile migratory mode (Caritas di Roma, 2002).

Most Senegalese migrants are *Wolof,* come mainly from the capital, the groundnut basin and the northwestern regions of Senegal, and belong to the *Mouride* Sufi Brotherhood. This was an order founded in the 1880s by Cheik Amadou Bamba, who gathered disciples from different strata of society (Cruise O'Brien, 1971; Copans, 1980; Piga, 2000). The Mouride Brotherhood has its capital in Touba, a city in which the Mourides built the largest mosque in sub-Saharan Africa and which remains a centre for its disciples' material and spiritual investments. Several studies have shown how the Brotherhood's vertical and horizontal ties also facilitated the development of social networks in migration and economic activities (Diop, 1985; Schmidt Friedberg, 1994; Scidà, 1994; Carter, 1997). The economic activity involving many Senegalese is street selling, although nowadays there are more cases of insertion in the labour market with regular employment, sometimes with jobs requiring high qualifications. Yet, many studies reveal direct or indirect experience of trade (cf. Ceschi, 1998). The Mourides, who historically moved from the rural environment, where they held the monopoly of groundnut production, to the urban environment, where they gradually acquired the monopoly of trade and informal transportation, are now involved in trade at various levels, from street-selling to the development of transnational electronic trade (Ebin, 1992).

Transnational spaces are kept alive by oral conversation: by telephone, as much as by people constantly moving from the sending and receiving contexts, and the selling of cassettes with recordings of sacred poems and information about decisions from the Touba establishment. The use of the Internet among some circles, which is widespread throughout the world, is another example of the brotherhood's ability to exploit new technologies to articulate its organisation cutting across geographical and political boundaries.

Studies focused on the Mouride trade diaspora in different contexts stress the power of the self-sustaining system of networks linking ties of belonging and trade. Although the existence of these linkages is beyond question, the networks of belonging and the trading networks do not automatically overlap, but help to develop each other (Salem, 1981). Moreover, Mouride networks are not closed systems with rigid boundaries; sometimes followers of other brotherhoods as well as students and workers, also rely on these trade networks to supplement their incomes. Often belonging to ethnic and religious groups is tempered in favour of a regional or national solidarity.

If one considers the partial opening of transnational networks, a further important aspect emerges in the understanding of transnational migration, i.e. the link between migrants and the access to power within the sending country. In a recent contribution, Salzbrunn shows how the current Senegalese President Wade, before winning the 2000 elections, focused on the influence of migrants over their relatives within the sending context, resulting in his being successful in obtaining the majority of the votes of the electors. "The strategy of sighting at transnational connections as votes multiplier has created an important economic mobilisation of political supporters" (Salzbrunn, 2002: 141). This is an example of how transnational migration does not necessarily mean non-national, but of how, vice-versa, it can be functional to the conquest of the nation-state.

The state's relevance is also evident when we turn our attention towards the receiving context. In the first place, only when a permit to stay in the country has been obtained is it then possible to practise a transnational life strategy, acting as a commuter crossing nation state boundaries. This simple fact should lead us to mitigate the post-national predictions of the authors mentioned in the previous section, and to acknowledge that transnational communities are nevertheless obliged to negotiate with the power the state exerts over territorial borders.

Some migrants remember their first arrival in the receiving context as an experience of patience and fatigue, waiting for the right moment to tempt fate. If and when they enter states, the Senegalese, as do other migrants, have to face numerous troubles. The shared representation of migrants as criminals, by which being irregular means being illegal, has implied the formation of an ever-growing segment of society that is frightened, with no legal protection, without any defence against greedy employers or landlords who see them as a chance for exploitation. This is the reality of individuals who are excluded from the society they live in. Furthermore, there are difficulties arising from a post-Fordist restructured economy and from the transformations implied by the disparate social politics adopted in different receiving countries. In addition to the disappointment with that "services' archipelago" (Pazzagli, 2002), which implements the policies with regards to migrants and often represents "the goodies" from the migrant's point of view, interactions with other institutions, such as the police, often turn into bureaucratic abuse, if not blatant discriminations. Many people experience endless standing in queues and never-ending waiting to obtain the needed documentation to avoid the destiny of being a "non-person" (Dal Lago, 1999).

The anxiety usually induced by the daily confrontation with the discriminatory arbitrariness of bureaucracy procedures is multiplied for migrants, who do not have access to the informal acquaintances that Italian citizens can often use in their support. These experiences also influence the way Senegalese look at Italy. Diverse accounts attest to a daily life consisting of discriminatory police checks, as police officers tend to be ruthless with one of the most visible migrant communities, because of both their street-selling activities and their coloured skin. When complaining about this situation, informants also often describe a frustrating situation, compared to a somewhat idealised different European country, to point out Italy's failure to become a civil context for receiving migration. Indeed, while European integration influences its country members and pushes them towards a higher level of political harmonisation, national migration policies are still uneven within different historical contexts.

Ambivalent Italian migration policies within "Fortress Europe"

One observes a deep ambiguity in Italian immigration policies, which express the labour market's objective need for foreign labourers while there is a growing criminalisation of migrants, often represented as strangers to be expelled. In the 1980s, the reaction of the Italian government to the migration phenomenon reflected this ambiguity. On the one hand, it was stated that Italy did not wish to base its economic development on the use of foreign labour. On the other hand, Italy, it was declared, was ready to welcome migrants in the name of its democratic tradition and solidarity with the difficult economic situation of developing countries (Carter, 1997). Consequently, migrants were given the possibility of settling in Italy, but without any real political recognition of their status and needs.

In this context, until 1986 – when the first of three national laws (1986, 1990, 1998) was ratified – immigration was tackled in terms of public order and control, leaving social questions to the voluntary sector. Under the 1986 law, migrant women were treated as economically and juridically dependent on their husbands (Salih, 2003). Children under 18, spouses and economically dependent parents were admitted for family reunion reasons, after evidence of the economic status and type of accommodation occupied by the person seeking the reunion was provided. A spouse or child's *permesso di soggiorno* was linked to that of the person already residing in Italy and was valid for the same period. The second law, enacted in 1990, claimed that the number of immigrants Italy could accept should be determined with reference to the needs of the national economy and in accordance with European treaties. In practice, this meant that during the 1990s permission to enter Italy was granted only for family reunion reasons, to political refugees (mainly from former Yugoslavia), and to those who already held an employment contract in Italy. One should note the irony of policies that strengthen barriers against those seeking to work legally, and thus implicitly encourage illegal entry, in spite of vocal opposition to undocumented immigration.

A significant factor in the evolution of Italian policy has been the country's membership in the EU and the development of EU policies regarding immigration, integration, exclusion, and xenophobia. Immigration into Italy (and other countries of Southern Europe) contributed to growing concern at a European level about frontiers. From a political perspective, Italian governments of all political persuasions have had to demonstrate that they are not providing an easy point of entry: the accusation is that they are the "soft underbelly" of the European Union. Contrary to this view of Italy as functionally tolerating irregular migration, Sciortino argues that Italian migration control shows a clear and fairly consistent restrictive trend both in relation to new inflows and to immigrants already present. This has resulted in an exclusionary definition of social membership. An example of the move towards a regime of closure and exclusion was provided by the reform of the citizenship law in 1992, which made it easier for descendants of Italian emigrants to regain citizenship, but also much more difficult for immigrants to apply for naturalisation. With its increase in emphasis on *jus sanguinis*, this law shaped a "two-tier system for naturalization" with a distinction between EU and non-EU foreigners; it aimed at reducing the number of the latter entitled to apply for naturalization. The required period of continuous legal residence was increased from five to ten years (Sciortino, 1999: 255).

Despite the demand for migrants within an increasingly fragmented and flexible labour market, the Italian government has therefore continued to strengthen border controls under the pressure of the idea of a "Fortress Europe" sanctioned by the Schengen Agreement. The Italian contribution to the building of the Fortress Europe became even more apparent with the Dini decree on immigration at the end of 1995. This was the product of the populist strategy of the Northern League and the National Alliance and it divided the Left. It represented a turning point from past political unwillingness to have a visible public debate on issues concerning immigration, towards a blatant exclusionary policy. The decree proposed the following: regularisation for two years for employed immigrants; the expulsion of illegal and unemployed immigrants; the expulsion of non-EU citizens under suspicion of being "socially dangerous"; and the immigrant's duty at the frontier to show a medical certificate. These measures would have involved the sacking of many irregular workers by employers unwilling to pay national insurance contributions and the consequent increase of irregular unemployed immigrants. Furthermore, the Dini decree emphasised the hypocrisy of Italian immigration policy and the paradox that, although economic interests and demographic decline urge the state to operate in the direction of increasing the number of migrant women and men in Italy and to integrate them in the local economy, political opportunism and electoral needs push in the opposite direction, as expressed by the increasing restriction of legal immigration into the country (Salih, 2003).

Even the third law on immigration (1998) seemed to be characterised by this ambiguous co-existence of claims for the integration of immigrants on the one hand, and, on the other hand the efforts deployed for their expulsion via the criminalisation of illegal immigrants. It indicated that the integration of migrants already settled in Italy is contingent upon the state's capacity to prevent further (illegal) immigration. Every year a maximum quota of entries is established, which includes seasonal and permanent workers and family reunions. However, these laws have contributed to defining migrants' rights and to establishing some measures for their integration by guaranteeing all non-EU workers legally resident in Italy and their families complete equality of rights and treatment with Italian workers. At the same time, they recognise their right to obtain houses, attend schools, organise associations and maintain their cultural identities. However, a substantial discrepancy still exists between the formal definition of rights and their implementation. In most cases the rights to housing, work and healthcare remain theoretical. The 1998 law, however, perpetuates the criminalisation of illegal immigration by fixing severe punishments for people who encourage clandestine immigration, and by creating the so-called *centri di permanenza temporanea* (CPT) for illegal entrants. The present Bossi-Fini law (2002) is more consistent: it institutionalises a quasi-apartheid regime.

In its concern about protecting the frontier, Italian political discourse replicates that found in many other European countries. Throughout the 1990s, irregular migration has been the favourite subject of aggressive political campaigns, conducted not only by the extreme Right. This feature contributed to the politicisation of the migratory phenomenon, the growth of the anxiety towards its control, and the tendency of the media to represent migrants as a socio-cultural problem, without grasping the complexity and variety of migration (Colombo and Sciortino, 2002). The xenophobic climate engendered by this growing tension about the control of territorial frontiers has had a negative effect on the situation of the residents belonging to ethnic minorities of immigrant origin.

Consequently, culture and cultural belonging were increasingly politicised. Indeed, exclusionary practices are often legitimised by cultural reasons, shaping that "cultural fundamentalism" (Stolcke, 1995) that celebrates differences to justify inequalities, stimulating the new differentialist racism widespread in many European countries. This specific discursive strategy denies and at the same time phrases opposition to foreigners in terms of common sense themes such as law and order, governmental irresponsibility, defence of local economic interests and taxpayers' rights. As such, it tacitly legitimises popular hostility to immigrants by depicting it as the natural response of people protecting their territories. Implicitly, beyond these discourses one finds the representation of immigrants as incommensurably different, if not culturally inferior (Cole, 1997).

Other representations that sound problematic from other points of view, may affect personnel in charge of the implementation of civil rights and of policies towards what has been called the "archipelago of immigration" (Mottura, 1992). Across Europe, in country after country, region after region, town after town, one may observe a host of national, but in some ways most interesting of all, of local initiatives, some based on state institutions, some in non-governmental organisations, some with the assistance and participation of immigrants or ethnic minorities themselves, some without, which attempt to address the issue of living in plural societies (Grillo and Pratt, 2002). In the following section we will consider the specific sedentarism that originates from the policies towards migrants in order to show how the actors of the "civil society" reveal some characteristics usually associated with state practices. The transnational organisation of migrant groups needs to negotiate with the sedentarism of such actors, which present "state effects" (Trouillot, 2001) not necessarily pertaining directly to state institutions.

"Seeing like a State": the sedentarist view of transnational migration

In the following discussion, we will see that some organisations that implement policies established by the state can reproduce discursively this orientation towards sedentarisation. In other words, I will try to show how various organisations stemming from the third sector and the too often romanticised "civil society" are able, to rephrase Scott (1998), to "see like the state".

Housing is the most urgent problem and a requirement for all immigrants in Italy. Moreover, this remains a major concern of local policies regarding immigration (Bernardotti, 2001). Although the racist explanations of discrimination in the housing market, such as price devaluation, targets immigrants in general, Senegalese have more problems in finding flats than other ethnic groups because of the widespread image of them as being willing to overcrowd.

Nevertheless, the ability shown by some Senegalese to accept living in large groups with a certain degree of autonomy has been considered a fundamental aid in shaping the model for primary assistance. Yet, a recurring opinion within public services is the "need to jump towards a next stage of integration and migration policies". Such a change should also be connected with the increasing number of rejoining families and should lead to housing policies being more oriented to flats rather than to collective accommodation, leaving an increasing degree of autonomy for migrants in questions relating to rent, maintenance and other expenses.

However, transnational organisation and orientation towards return, typical of many Senegalese, fit more within the forms of "first reception" rather than in this "second stage towards integration". Therefore, from concrete everyday experiences emerges an image of the Senegalese that does not correspond to the sedentary logic implicitly informing the social services system, as well as integration policy planning. Senegalese are blamed from many quarters for their lack of identification with the receiving context and the symbolic and material orientation towards the sending one. Phrases such as "they're not identified with the place they live in", "they live thinking of their families in Senegal" occur frequently. Senegalese attachment towards their place of origin – along with their mobile and circular way of organising the migratory experience – is, therefore, seen as a problem. The sedentary way of life and its institutionalisation are also considered existential "data" for the working and bureaucratic practices they entail. The settlement and rooting of groups within a territory lived as "their own" is considered the normal condition, and is taken for granted as the sole existential solution, the natural reality of humankind (Callari Galli, 1998). The Senegalese, finally, are not "disciplined" enough. Ideal at the first reception stage, they are less and less so for the policies of integration, which are perceived as "worthy" only for those who show a strong desire to settle down permanently within the receiving context (Riccio, 2001).

Such sedentarism involves the migrants themselves, especially those considered representative of foreign communities. Drawing from Gledhill (1998: 6), I would argue that "states (and local governments) have learned ... how to bend the new politics of ethnic identities to their advantage by promoting institutional structures of representation and professional careers of intermediation for community leaders ... there seems to be an increase in the taxonomic, identity-fixing efforts of receiving states rather than a decrease". For instance, during the summer of 1997 some criminal events in which foreigners were involved produced a "migration alarm" at a national level rather than a "criminal alert" at a regional level. Criminality and migration came to be discussed as part of a unique social phenomenon. Since in the majority of those crimes the perpetrators came from other localities, the mayor of Rimini suggested a solution, which would be illegal from the point of view of European and international law: the closure of the province to foreign residents coming from other Italian provinces. In other words, the right to mobility would be ensured on a differential ethnic and national basis: a sort of apartheid, and not even an implicit one.

After this sedentary proposal, which in the end did not lead to any concrete decision, a press conference was called with the participation of those defined as

Transnational Migrations 87

"the representatives of the *extracomunitari* citizens". However, a detailed analysis of the meeting is not our concern here. I am interested only in showing some passages of the speech of a foreign citizen, who worked in a trade union, because they show how so-called "representatives" of migrants can assimilate the dominant sedentarism. Their function as representatives often emerges more from the interaction with the receiving institutions rather than from being an effective representation of the community of origin.

> "The problems during the summer are created by the people who come from outside, foreign residents have not even the time to go to the sea because they are here to work for the tourist season. ... It is important that we condemn those events, they are unacceptable and we are ready to collaborate with the local authorities to face these problems. We forwarded this proposal to the prefect in the provincial meeting for public security, which is to control the territory well through the policing of its points of entry: motorway, railway station and main highways. ... Every foreigner will be checked: What does he do? What are his intentions? We will ask the police that anyone who is found without means, without a clear residence permit, even if they are regular, I repeat even if they are regular, will have to be sent to their residential commune, or outside the province of Rimini anyway. In Rimini, we do not have problems. Problems start during the summer when people come from outside."

It is as if the need to legitimise themselves in the eyes of the Italian audience pushed some of these "foreigners' representatives" to reiterate the language of law and order one may find in the media and in the "new rhetoric of exclusion" (Stolcke, 1995) and to unwittingly contribute to the general criminalisation of migrants. The main theme stressed is that "problems come from outside". "Our immigrants", the ones we control, we know, we represent, we can number precisely, are good because we are doing a good job.

The continuous presence from different points of view of this sedentary and localistic view testify to the persistence of the effects of the "state effects", which go beyond the borders of traditionally defined state practices. Free from the need to affirm its end, or, on the other hand, its endlessness, we should focus our analyses on the multiple ongoing transformations that characterise state practices and are implemented through other organisations as well (Ferguson and Gupta 2002). These processes emerge strongly from the confrontation with new transnational migrations.

Concluding reflections: translocal and institutional ethnography

This path leads us to steer between two positions. On the one hand, I take a cautious attitude towards exclusively state-centred theories of migration, precisely because both the migrant communities and the sending and receiving societies are showing greater independence from sending and receiving states. On the other hand, I recognise that the exclusionary and disciplinary power of states is far from fading. It seems difficult to think that the development of transnational connections will make the existence of the nation state and its rhetoric redundant. The analyses that acknowledge the continuing importance of nation states and their influence on transnational social and political fields are an important corrective to celebratory and premature assertions that this is the era of the decline of "modern" institutions. While recognising the complexity and fluidity of contemporary identities and cultures, I am led to refute such claims.

State control and migrants' transnational practices constitute interactive parts of the same picture. Political and hegemonic interpretations of the migrant as "other" at the national level, and his or her marginalisation in the host country, interact with migrants' strategies and their construction of identities that challenge national discourses by extending beyond national boundaries. Transnational experiences and trajectories are profoundly anchored in the material, legal and cultural constraints and possibilities that grow out of the local and national places where migrants live. Consequently, sending and receiving contexts shape migrants' transnational experiences and projects in many different ways. Thus, transnational practices may be highly embedded within nation-building processes, and saying transnational is not as saying post-national.

The state, national as much as local, is not, of course, a monolithic entity, but rather a composite of different agencies with potentially contrasting interests. As Abélès points out (2001: 42), "every institution is torn by tensions" and the aim of ethnographers is to highlight, "taking the representations of his informants as a starting point, the sometimes heteroclite logic, their overlapping, the gaps which they induce". Consequently, discourses and practices of migration can be at odds with each other within state institutions.

Overall, however, I believe that in receiving societies the role of nation states has not declined in fields such as immigration, and that in sending societies the nation state continues to play a crucial role in shaping and creating transnational political and economic fields, reflecting an increasing dependency on migrants' remittances (Smith, 1998). Therefore, in receiving and sending societies alike the state forms part of the material, economic and normative conditions, impinging on migrants' transnational practices and shaping their lived experience of transnationality. This is highlighted by how rights to citizenship are distributed and access to resources are differentiated. Citizenship in Italy is still linked to nationality and non-citizens are in principle denied access to the public sphere, as it is defined by the state. In Italy, an exclusionary politics of difference operates to prevent migrants from actually accessing citizenship. The material and normative conditions of uncertainty under which many migrants live their lives impinge upon both their socio-economic strategies and the construction of their social personhood within a transnational field. Therefore, it becomes vital to reflect further on the relation between the national and the transnational by deepening the understanding of how transnational identities and practices are articulated with migrants' rights at the national level.

Finally, from a methodological point of view, to adopt a non state-centred approach does not mean to remove the state and its transformations from the analysis. I hope that I have highlighted the fragmented and heterogeneous nature of transnational practices and identifications, revealing the complexity of transnationality as a phenomenon that continuously negotiates with public and state-like institutions. Rather than being a uniform process, transnationality is a complex and varied terrain, experienced differently according to sending contexts, class, and gender (Riccio, 2000, 2002; Koser, 2000; Salih, 2003). It is of particular concern to uncover the articulation between institutional structures and migrants' practices in shaping transnational forms of life, by deepening a multi-dimensional understanding of how these processes evolve (Grillo, 2001). Such an approach highlights a specific embeddedness within nation states' hegemony, which often forges different experiences of transnationality.

References

ABÉLÈS, M. 2001: Politica, gioco di spazi. Roma: Meltemi.
AMIT-TALAI, V. 1998: Risky Hiatuses and the Limits of Social Imagination: Expatriancy in the Cayman Islands. In: N. Rapport, A. Dawson (eds.), Migrants of Identity. Oxford: Berg.
ANDERSON, B. 1996: Comunità immaginate. Origini e diffusione dei nazionalismi. Roma: Manifestolibri.
APPADURAI, A. 1996: Modernity at Large. Cultural Dimension of Globalization. Minneapolis: Minnesota University Press.
BASCH, L. GLICK SCHILLER, N., SZANTON-BLANC, C. 1994: Nations Unbound: Transnational Projects, Postcolonial Predicaments, and Deterritorialized Nation-States. New York: Gordon and Breach.
BERNARDOTTI, M. A. (ed.) 2001: Con la valigia accanto al letto. Immigrati e casa a Bologna. Milano: Franco Angeli.
CALLARI GALLI, M. 1998: I percorsi della complessità umana. In: M. Callari Galli, M. Ceruti, T. Pievani, Pensare la diversità. Roma: Meltemi.
CALLARI GALLI, M. 2003: I nomadismi della contemporaneità. In: M. Callari Galli (ed.), Nomadismi contemporanei. Rimini: Guaraldi.
CARITAS DI ROMA 2002: Immigrazione: dossier statistico 2002. Roma: Anterem.
CARTER, D. M. 1997: States of Grace. Senegalese in Italy and the New European Immigration. Minneapolis: University of Minnesota Press.
CESCHI, S. 1998: Spazi culturali dei venditori ambulanti della comunità senegalese a Roma. In: P. Clemente, A. M. Sobrero (eds.), Persone dall'Africa. Roma: CISU.
CLIFFORD, J. 1997: Routes. Travel and Translation in the Late Twentieth Century. Cambridge, Mass.: Harvard University Press.

COLE, J. 1997: The New Racism in Europe: a Sicilian Ethnography. Cambridge: Cambridge University Press.
COLOMBO A., SCIORTINO G. (eds.) 2002: Stranieri in Italia. Assimilati ed esclusi. Bologna: Il Mulino.
COPANS, J. 1980: Les Marabouts de l'arachide: la confrérie mouride et les paysans du Sénégal. Paris: Le Sycomore.
CRUISE O'BRIEN, D. B. 1971: The Mourides of Senegal. The Political and Economic Organisation of an Islamic Brotherhood. Oxford: Clarendon Press.
DAL LAGO, A. 1999: Non-persone. L'esclusione dei migranti in una società globale. Milano: Feltrinelli.
DIOP, A. M. 1985: Les Associations Murid en France. In: Esprit, n. 102.
DIOP, M. C. (ed.) 2002: Le Sénégal contemporain. Paris: Karthala.
EBIN, V. 1992: A la recherche de nouveaux "poissons". Stratégies commerciales mourides par temps de crise. In: Politique Africaine, n. 45.
EPSTEIN, A. L. 1958: Politics in an Urban African Community. Manchester: Manchester University Press.
FERGUSON, J., GUPTA, A. 2002: Spatializing States: toward an Ethnography of Neoliberal Governamentality. In: American Ethnologist, vol. 29, n. 4.
GLEDHILL, J. 1998: Thinking about States, Subalterns and Power Relations in a World of Flows. In: ICCCR International Conference on Transnationalism (Manchester 17 May).
GLICK SCHILLER, N., BASCH, L., SZANTON-BLANC, C. (ed.) 1992: Toward a Transnational Perspective on Migration. New York: New York Academy of Science.
GRILLO, R. D. 1973: African Railwayman. Solidarity and Opposition in an African Labour Force. Cambridge: Cambridge University Press.
GRILLO, R. D. (ed.) 1980: "Nation" and "State" in Europe: Anthropological Perspectives. London: Academic Press.
GRILLO, R. D. 2000: Riflessioni sull'approccio transnazionale alle migrazioni. In: Afriche e orienti, vol. 2, n. 3/4.
GRILLO, R. D. 2001: Transnationalism and the City: Anthropological Perspectives. In: C. Cellamare, B. Riccio (eds.), Plural Cities, monographic issue of Plurimondi, n. 5.
GRILLO, R. D., PRATT, J. (eds.) 2002: The Politics of Recognizing Difference. Multiculturalism Italian-style. Aldershot: Ashgate.
GUPTA, A., Ferguson, J. (eds.) 1997: Culture, Power, Place. Durham: Duke University Press.
HANNERZ, U. 1996: Transnational Connections. London: Routledge.
KEARNEY, M. 1996: Reconceptualizing the Peasantry. Anthropology in Global Perspective. Boulder: Westview Press.
KOSER, K. 2000: Da rifugiati a comunità transnazionali? Il caso eritreo in Inghilterra e Germania. In: Afriche e orienti, vol. 2, n. 3/4.
MACGAFFEY, J., BAZENGUISSA-GANGA, R. 2000: Congo-Paris. Transnational Traders on the Margins of the Law. Bloomingto: Indiana University Press.

MOTTURA, G. (ed.) 1992: L'arcipelago immigrazione. Roma: Ediesse.
ONG, A. 1999: Flexible Citizenship. The Cultural Logics of Transnationality. Durham: Duke University Press.
PARKIN, D. 1969: Neighbours and Nationals in an African City Ward. London: Routledge.
PAZZAGLI I. G. 2002: L'arcipelago dei servizi: uno sguardo sulle dimensioni organizzative. In: A. Sgrignuoli (ed.), Donne migranti dall'accoglienza alla formazione. Un'analisi culturale dentro e fuori i servizi. Milano: Franco Angeli.
PIGA, A. 2000: Dakar e gli ordini Sufi. Roma: Bagatto.
RICCIO, B. 2000: Spazi transnazionali: esperienze senegalesi. In: Afriche e orienti, vol. 2, n. 3/4.
RICCIO, B. 2001: Migranti senegalesi e operatori sociali nella Riviera romagnola. Una etnografia multi-vocale del fenomeno migratorio. In: La ricerca folklorica, n. 44.
RICCIO, B. 2002: Senegal is Our Home: the Anchored Nature of Senegalese Transnational Networks. In: N. Al-Ali, K. Koser (eds.), New Approaches to Migration? Transnational Communities and the Transformation of Home. London: Routledge.
ROSSI, C. 2003: Antropologia culturale. Appunti di metodo per la ricerca nei "mondi contemporanei". Milano: Guerini.
ROUSE, R. 1991: Mexican Migration and the Social Space of Postmodernism. In: Diaspora, vol. 1, n. 1.
SALEM, G. 1981: De la brousse sénégalaise au Boul' Mich: le système commercial mouride en France. In: Cahiers d'Etudes Africaines, n. 81-83.
SALIH, R. 2003: Gender in Transnationalism, Plurinational Subjects: Identity, Migration and Difference among Moroccan Women in Italy. London: Routledge.
SALZBRUNN, M. 2002: L'impatto delle reti transnazionali degli emigrati sulle elezioni presidenziali in Senegal nel 2000. In: Afriche e orienti, vol. 4, n. 4.
SCHMIDT DI FRIEDBERG, O. 1994: Islam, solidarietà e lavoro. I muridi senegalesi in Italia. Torino: Edizioni della Fondazione Agnelli.
SCIDÀ, G. 1994: Fra carisma e clientelismo: una confraternita musulmana in migrazione. In: Studi Emigrazione/Etudes Migrations, vol. 31, n. 113.
SCIORTINO, G. 1999: Mapping in the Dark: The Evolution of Italian Immigration Control. In: G. Brochman, T. Hammar (eds.), Mechanisms of Immigration Control. Oxford: Berg.
SCOTT, J. C. 1998: Seeing Like a State. How Certain Schemes to Improve the Human Condition Have Failed. New Haven: Yale University Press.
SMITH, M. P., GUARNIZO, L. E. (eds.) 1998: Transnationalism from Below. New Brunswick: Transaction Publishers.
SMITH, R. C. 1998: Transnational Localities: Community, Technology and the Politics of Membership within the Context of Mexico and U.S. Migration.

In: M. P. Smith, L. E. Guarnizo (eds.), Transnationalism from Below. New Brunswick: Transaction Publishers.

STOLCKE V. 1995: New Boundaries, New Rhetorics of Exclusion in Europe. In: Current Anthropology, n. 36.

TROUILLOT, M.-R. 2001: The Anthropology of the State in the Age of Globalization. In: Current Anthropology, vol. 42, n. 1.

VERTOVEC, S. 1999: Conceiving and Researching Transnationalism. In: Ethnic and Racial Studies, vol. 2, n. 2.

Humanitarian Contexts and Emergent Peripheries: International Cooperation and Contemporary Nomadism

Ivo Giuseppe Pazzagli

Premise

The new nomadisms in contemporary life have become a prominent and emerging object of research and cultural reflection (Bhabha, 1994; Appadurai, 1996; Hannerz, 1996). Among the new actors of this world, that is both fragmented and crossed by transnational flows, we must certainly include the operators who in various ways move along the several paths created by humanitarian intervention and international cooperation (Fisher, 1997; Markowitz, 2001; Mehta, 2001; Pandolfi, 2000). On the other hand, the world of humanitarian intervention and cooperation is a complex and vast archipelago nowadays, which has been developing progressively since the end of the Second World War; it is one of the phenomena that mark the complex dynamics characterising globalisation processes (Fisher, 1997; Markowitz, 2001; Mehta, 2001).

One of the peculiarities and effects of globalisation is the production it entails of new forms of nomadism and "intentional" cultural hybridism. As I shall illustrate further referring to the case of former Yugoslavia, humanitarian intervention and international cooperation, which contribute to the construction of contexts characterised by the weaving and comparison of logics, representations, and interests of various social players, entail activating negotiation, mediation and cultural hybridisation processes; therefore, they are the object of growing attention for anthropologists (Fisher, 1997; Markowitz, 2001; Mehta, 2001).

The complexity of the new contexts

As many anthropologists have underlined within the debates of recent years, the processes related to globalisation, accelerating the circulation of people, information, images and meanings, contribute to the production of diversity. Processes such as the creation of transnational and delocalised cultures – or, as Hannerz (1992: 249) defines them, "structures of meaning carried by social networks, which are not wholly based in any single territory" – on the one side, and hybridisation and indigenisation processes on the other, are not a prelude to a reduction of diversity. Conversely, they lead to its accelerated production and to a profound transformation of the processes characterising the making and exposure of such diversities through the intertwining of the local and the global, as well as a transformation of the ways in which individuals and groups use such differences in diverse local and global arenas where they interact.

The globalisation of contexts, on the other hand, provides a new, larger scene of action, not only for the new waves of identity, for the desperate affirmations of professed ethnic, religious or historical peculiarities, or even for the recursive and extreme manifestations of symbolic, intellectual and physical violence, but also for the numerous actors moving within the arenas periodically activated by international crises. And the impossibility of controlling the consequences of social action obliges us to be increasingly attentive to the complexity of the fields that structure themselves within the connection of the local and the global within such scenes (Agier, 1997).

Anthropology and development cooperation

The implication of anthropology in development cooperation and in projects of planned adjustment is well established and at the same time has always been an issue of controversy and debates within the discipline.

Since the sixties, the anthropology of development, direct progeny of applied anthropology, has been able to reach a relative autonomy to become eventually an independent branch (Colajanni, 1994, 1998).

Such a situation is probably due, as Borofsky states (1994: 413), to the always clear and subjacent continuity of subjects of study generally preferred by the anthropologists: "losers" or "left behind", anthropology has always devoted a particular attention to those who have less power, to those at the margins, rather than at the core of political and economic Western power. This could be because, since the second half of the nineteenth century, the diverse forms of relation established between "us" and the "others" have seen used nearly continuously at the frontier,[1] more or less implied and more or less conscious of the complex power relations that the "developed" Western society has in dealing with the other in the forms of colonialism and neo-colonialism (Hymes, 1969; Malighetti, 2002). Indeed, anthropology's involvement in the transformation processes of the people of the world's south has been constant and has even taken on very different modalities from time to time.

In practical terms, the anthropologist has been playing different yet interconnected roles: collecting and analysing information, giving support in defining projects and politics, participating in the realisation of such projects and monitoring the effects in terms of social and cultural change (Nolan, 2002). Such direct implication has been rooted in the belief that a selective use of anthropological

---

[1] For an interpretation of anthropology as knowledge of frontier, because developed in areas of contact and exchange between different cultures, see Fabietti 1999.

knowledge can become an advantage related to the improvement of the conditions of the groups towards which interventions are directed, as well as to a major efficacy of the interventions themselves. Yet, although such an attitude is widely shared among those anthropologists involved in cooperation actions, there is no agreement as to the ways such knowledge should be used for the best (Gow, 2002; Colajanni, 1994, 1998).

On the one side, Cernea, an anthropologist who has been employed for several years at the World Bank, is positioned in a way he himself defines as the *social engineering action model*. He argues for transposing social science knowledge into tools of knowledge and change in order to produce and organise new social relations, as well as to democratise the planning processes and to facilitate a broader participation (1991, 1995). As Gow underlines (2002), Cernea proposes a contemporary version of "anthropological authority" when he states that the social scientist, and only he, is the person in the position of being able to decide and to talk as the representative of local people.

On the opposite side is the standpoint expressed by Alan Hoben (1982), maybe the first anthropologist who has held an important position in USAID, the agency of the US federal government for development and humanitarian intervention: he has also been one of the pioneers in writing about the experience of anthropological fieldwork within development institutions (Gow, 2002). In his view, anthropology can play an important role contributing to clarify and transform many of the explicit and implicit assumptions that are at the core of the actions of those responsible for the planning and implementation of development actions and humanitarian interventions (Hoben, 1982). This critical function can be explicated through a work of clarification aimed at the transformation of the perspectives of the actors involved; this approach is thus designed to give a bottom-up vision of development processes, trying to highlight the nature of organisations, interests and strategies of local elites and bureaucracies. Such a methodological orientation is built around the notion of "elucidation" and on a faith in education processes. It is a strategy aware of the need to put into practice a cluttered, uncertain and slow course to obtain some results in society in terms of change. This approach is opposed to the propulsion towards action, the hierarchical and decisional character of the *social engineering action model* (Gow, 2002).

Yet, above and beyond the diversity of such approaches and the scarce tendency to communicate the results of this professional work, the contribution of anthropologists has invested numerous issues: from the processes of forced relocation to colonialism, from the study of organisation and the characters of local elites to the knowledge of family economies and systems of communal properties, from the study of formal economies to that of informal economies (Gow 2002: 203).

From an anthropology engaged in development processes to an anthropology of development

Notwithstanding the inevitable contiguity and reciprocal frequentation in the fields, there has not been a great feeling either between anthropologists and representatives of various colonial administrations at first, and then with the bureaucrats of international organisations, or between the anthropologists engaged in development projects and those working in academia (Escobar, 1995; Gow, 2002; Malighetti, 2002).

If on the one hand this could be understood in terms of the poor practical outcomes of the several attempts at collaboration due to the "not easily commensurability between anthropological knowledge and that reputed necessary by *practical people*" (Malighetti, op. cit., 98), on the other, the compromising, implicit dimension relating to any research with concrete goals, developed within strongly asymmetrical and not easily classifiable power relations such as those between the industrialised West and the so-called *underdeveloped* countries during their de-colonisation phase, constituted a problem.

Furthermore, in the mid-eighties, under the influence of the prevalent de-constructional and post-modern approaches, anthropology engaged in the field of development cooperation projects was subjected to a caustic and radical critique together with cooperation in its complexity; the major accusation was that it was simply an advanced form of neo-colonialism and imperialism. And it is within the framework of this radical criticism – which attempts to state the existence of a substantial *historical continuity* between the *westernising* practices of planned change peculiar to the colonial period and the contemporary initiatives for the development of ex-colonial countries – that, according to some authors, the implication of a segment of anthropology from the second half of the twentieth century in the development projects and initiatives set up in ex-colonial countries needs to be interpreted (Grillo, Rew 1985; Escobar, 1995; Malighetti, 2002).

This is an anathema of sorts that the new *Development Anthropology* launched against the practices articulated around the development cooperation field and the anthropology that *committed* itself to it.

According to Gow, the anthropologist who most of all and above all has contributed to launching the post-modern challenge to the relationship between anthropology and development has been Escobar (1991, 1995), who through the years has staunchly stated his theses, regardless of the critical barrier posed by other anthropologists (Tommasoli, 2001).

Nonetheless, his critique has brought the anthropological community, as well as those anthropologists highly committed to the field of cooperation and humanitarian intervention, to reflect on the notion of development itself and to raise the level of analysis to include in the field of enquiry the role and characters of the organisations involved to various extents in intervention, such as international organisations, NGOs, media, movements as well as the languages, intended more as a productive machine of realities rather than as an instrument able to reflect the "real" (Fisher, 1997; Hudson, 2001; Markowitz, 2001; Mehta, 2001; Pandolfi, 2002; Sabelli, 1994).

Taking a Focauldian perspective as a starting point, the notion of development has been examined as a discursive practice systematically related to forms of knowledge and techniques of power. Within such a perspective, the discourse of development could work to justify and legitimise an intervention aimed at introducing a transformation imposed from the outside and whose supposed "necessity" is based on a pre-definition of both the problem and the modes of solution (Gow, 2002; Mehta, 2001).

Such a critique is intertwined and progressively reconnected, on one side, to the more general debate on cultural transformations related to globalisation processes and the crisis of modernity, and on the other to the responses that such changes produce within the anthropological debate. The latter reached its highest point of acceleration in the years immediately after the publication in 1986 of the book *Writing Culture: Poetics and Politics of Ethnography*, edited by George Marcus and James Clifford, comprising the essays and reflections that emerged during a series of seminars held in 1984 at the School of American Research in Santa Fe, New Mexico. A book that has divided anthropology, and shed light on problems, doubts and critiques present for a long time in the anthropological debate (Clifford, Marcus, 1986; Callari Galli, 2000, p. 65; Hymes, 1969) and which has not left intact any of the old certainties on which ethnographic work was rooted.

The new scenarios of cooperation and the role of the NGOs
Undoubtedly, anthropology has not been the only discipline obliged to radically revise its theoretical and methodological coordinates under the pressure of the economic and political changes characterising the last quarter of the past century. Since the end of the partition into two opposed blocs, symbolised by the fall of the Berlin Wall, and up to the acceleration in the development of new information and communication technologies, the eighties to some extent constitute a clear break between the politics and intervention strategies adopted in the aftermath of the Second World War by the super-powers emerging as winners of the conflict and the politics elaborated later on with the dissolution of the two blocs. Against this background of general changes, in the late eighties the crisis of the intervention models used until then within development cooperation practices emerges in all its evidence. The nineties, in fact, are characterised by the research of new paths and strategies of development. Since the 1992 Summit on Earth in Rio de Janeiro organised by the UN, the last decade of the twentieth century is constellated with the subsequent international conferences organised by the UN and with the multiplication of forums and international conferences organised by NGOs, which contribute to place the focus on this crisis and to define new orientations and frames of reference in order to build up and manage interventions (Ianni, 1999).

In this new scenario, NGOs took on an increasing position in the management of resources addressed to development projects. This phenomenon played a major role in transforming the diverse arenas of development cooperation in contexts inhabited by an increasing number of different actors.

From the specific point of view of contemporariness interpreted in its nomadic aspects, three aspects of this process are worth highlighting for their relevance.

Firstly, the growth of the importance of the NGOs' role in cooperation processes pushed the donors towards a major formalisation of the politics they intended to pursue and of the procedures of resource allocation as well as management and control of the projects, when not imposing the logic of the knowledge of reality and of *problem setting* considered to be *scientific and universal*. This has often safeguarded the definition of action strategies from any contamination or valorisation of the systems of knowledge and interpretation of reality linked to the specificities of local cultures (Metha, 2001). This process drove the NGOs themselves towards the more or less conscious assumption of formalising logic and the adoption of intervention methodologies relatively disconnected from the peculiarity of each specific context of intervention, as they were obliged to move within a sort of translocal *technoscape* (Appadurai, 1996).

Secondly, it is relevant to mention the role NGOs played over the last fifteen years in activating movements in support of their activities. In fact, besides elaborating specific and peculiar organisational cultures, NGOs are often the expression of movements or social organisations with specific value orientations, when not embodying ideological, political and/or religious options. In such a perspective therefore, they have been and are still playing an active role, interpreting and giving concrete meaning to the notion of development, interpretations and ideas whose diffusion is often promoted by NGOs themselves, thus favouring the birth of the movement sustaining their action.[2] In other words, the last few years witnessed the growing commitment of NGOs, both in the North and the South of the world, active in cooperation for development and humanitarian aid, in constructing networks interconnecting various geographical areas and sociocultural milieus in different ways in order to facilitate the circulation of important flows of resources and people, information and ideologies, scientific knowledge and technologies.

Finally, during the nineties, we witness the establishment of another process in the framework of cooperation for development and humanitarian aid: the so-called de-centred cooperation (Ianni, 1999). In France and Italy especially there has been a rapid growth of experience involving the participation of new sub-

---

[2] Markowitz (2001) notes that in Latin America, by encouraging the formation of vast groups sustaining their action, NGOs have been playing a critical role in the formation of social movements contributing to revitalising and expanding civil society and even reaching the level of a discrete influence in directing the destination of resources, reaching in the end the capacity of playing a visible and formal role in political life.

jects: from voluntary associations to unions and local administrations, to recreational company clubs. Within a framework characterised by a mounting and ever severe critique of the logic and strategies of the traditional twofold development cooperation, we witness the affirmation of a rhetoric emphasising categories of seemingly *"alternative"* nature.

New bywords such as *co-development, participative development, decentred cooperation, bottom-up development,* often put in opposition to the state on one side and civil society on the other, legitimise and provide an ideological framework to a vision of cooperation, which Ralph Grillo and Bruno Riccio (2004) define as *populist,* and which provides the prime support to the activation of a multiplicity of actors within micro-projects, both in the homeland – especially when dealing with migrant communities – and within underdeveloped countries.

These projects quite often activate bi-directional floods, since they tend to involve groups of migrants in development projects of the local contexts they come from, suggesting a sort of twinning between local communities, or aiming at objectives not only limited to the activation of money and *know-how* between *here* and *there,* but also to the building-up of a reciprocal knowledge throughout different forms: from the reciprocal visits of local authorities to hospitality given to children, to forms of responsible tourism, and so forth.

In addition, these three phenomena, as Callari Galli underlines in her introduction, are not only intertwined in a framework characterised by the progressive weakening of the equivalence of culture and territory in favour of the diffusion of general ideas, lifestyles and belonging to imagined communities increasingly typified by territorial multi-polarities, but also involve individuals and groups – migrants and refugees, urban masses marked by extreme poverty and street children just to mention a few examples, whose relation with the territory appears profoundly altered in different ways.

The new contexts of cooperation and humanitarian intervention: the case of former Yugoslavia

The concomitant and synergic action of these three factors, made possible by globalisation processes in economics and communication, has in fact made the "field" of cooperation and humanitarian intervention much more complex than it was in the past. And this complexity imposes, for the sake of analysis, paying attention to a multiplicity of variables, contexts and plans, which intertwine diversely in concrete situations.

In order to offer you a concrete example of the complexity of the field, I will refer to the Balkan context, which has deeply involved Italy all through the last decade. The experience of the Balkan war is, in my opinion, a very good example of how globalisation processes interact in the dynamics of humanitarian interventions and development cooperation. Such processes also contribute to structure contexts characterised by the weaving and confrontation of logic, representations and the interests of social actors, more numerous and diverse than in the past.

I choose ex-Yugoslavia as an example not only because of the deep involvement of our country in its context, but also because of its evident paradigmatic character in relation to the question I am dealing with.

Much literature of diverse disciplines, in fact, has focused its attention on the new and dramatically original elements emerging in the Balkan area before, during and immediately after the crisis.

The ex-Yugoslavia experience, on the other hand, having been the first international crisis in the aftermath of the dissolution of the two blocs, has had an absolutely peculiar and paradigmatic character because it concentrates and contains a multiplicity of processes, which have never before appeared simultaneously; undeniably, it represents a watershed between old and new emergencies.

The Balkan crisis has indeed represented an unattended and shocking novelty, since it revealed how forms of conflict tribalism, considered until then as a peculiar exclusivity of "other" and faraway contexts from a spatial and a political-cultural point of view alike, could explode in the inner heart of Europe. The crisis dramatically showed how illusory was the conviction that school education and political participation could, per se, constitute an adequate boundary against barbarity. Though the Balkans have always been considered *Europe's powder keg*, a *boundary marker* for centuries under the influence of a non-European culture, Tito's ex-Yugoslavia had also been the cradle of the *non-aligned countries* and the first socialist country to distance itself from Stalinism and the politics of the opposed blocs, feeding the illusion, both in the North and in the South of the world, that *socialism with a human face* was possible. A surprise and disenchantment, which certainly influenced the time before the rest of Europe became aware of the ongoing drama.

On the other hand, the paradigmatic character of such an experience is confirmed by the vast literature emerging in the last few years, and which, directly or indirectly, refers to the Balkan crisis: from the war newspaper reports to the literature featuring a diary-type and/or first-hand reflections[3] concerning the post-war phase, to scientific contributions from various disciplines developed in the conflict's immediate aftermath. In fact, the attention of much of the anthropologically-based literature has been broadly focused on all the new and dramatically original situations produced in the Balkan area before, during and immediately after the crisis: the collapse of the state and the conflict's ethnicisation; the ethnic cleansing (Nagengast, 1994; Hayden, 2002); the military intervention of the multinational force and the humanitarian intervention of international organs, with the suspension of sovereignty, which, especially in the di-

---

[3] Purely as an example of this type of literature see Canevaro, Berlini, Camasta, 1998; Mattioli, 1999. I would like to thank specially Alfredo Camerini, whose long-term experience in different contexts and various roles reveal itself of enormous importance in enhancing my understanding of the subject here discussed.

rect post-emergency phase, it seems to entail (Campbell, 1999; Ignatieff, 2002; Pandolfi, 2000, 2002); and last, the new role taken on by the media in the construction and management of the Yugoslavian crisis and humanitarian crises in general (Both, 2001; Appadurai, 1996, 2002).

Furthermore, in these years the Balkans have been and still are the object of interventions of humanitarian nature and of development cooperation with many varied typologies and dimensions. Such projects have put into confrontation and woven together stories of people, small organisations, large international institutions and local communities.[4]

Still, without detriment to the important acquisitions that have matured in this debate, the angle from which I find it interesting to analyse the Balkan events, from the viewpoint of nomadism, is that of studying and connecting the various "arenas" (the Italian and the Balkan) enacted by the crisis with the intent of grasping the transforming processes that affected the various players involved.

The events of ex-Yugoslavia have in fact increased the number and type of people who have directly experienced the context of a humanitarian crisis and have involved a broad base of non-professional cooperation.

The reasons for the involvement of unusual groups and players are grounded in the peculiarity of the conflict in ex-Yugoslavia. There are many and can be found in the plurality of elements of representation and experience which it has given echo to.

The Italian scene in relation to the Balkan crisis
For many years, Yugoslavia was a well-known and familiar place to Italians, associated with a tourist imaginary as well as with precise and direct holiday experiences.

Against this background, the outbreak of the war in Croatia in 1990, as documented by the considerable literature on this subject that has appeared in past years, seemed to many not only unexpected and unexplainable, but also something that could be set in a place that many had experienced and whose representation contrasted dramatically with the conflict's images provided by the media.

On the other hand, the war's outbreak immediately entailed the arrival in Italy of a disorderly and sometimes frantic flow of refugees, who have contributed to making the consequences of the conflict even more concrete through the stories of direct witnesses.

With Italy fully immersed in an institutional crisis and crossed by the rising of the Northern League, the media's unrestrainable involvement on the scene of a bloody and fratricidal conflict, geographically close and perceived as within the

---

[4] As the players involved in these events are mainly organisational players, on a methodological level, besides the consolidated anthropological fieldwork approaches, I will also refer to the narrative approach applied to the study of organisations and organisational culture (Fabietti, 1999; Carniawska, 1997).

European context – its connection not only with the transition from a state-controlled economy to a market economy, but also with the crisis of a country that had always appeared to be the most Western one among Eastern Europe's – surely conjured up, during those years, the ghosts and worries on the domestic front and required the taking on of responsibilities of associations, political organisations and institutional operators. Therefore, solidarity and humanitarian intervention, also thanks to the coverage offered by the media, became a very peculiar arena in which various players staged a complex, polysemic performance, aimed at a variety of audiences in which – and this is the hypothesis of my work – by virtue of the complexity of the field that was progressively being structured, the identity of professional groups traditionally involved in humanitarian interventions, as well as that of players who appeared on this scene for the first time, was transformed.

Even for citizens less involved in voluntary and humanitarian action, there were many occasions in which some forms of direct contact with aspects of these dramatic and complicated events were possible: from the caravans of indiscriminate and chaotic humanitarian aid unfolded at the height of the conflict under the emphatic spotlights of the national and local press (Miozzo, 1998), to the countless volunteer associations activated in the post-war period in the most varied areas, to the local institutions that intervened immediately in a subsequent phase to follow, cover and give political expression to civil society's activism through the so-called "decentred cooperation".

We have reached a point where the Balkan crisis becomes an emblematic example from different points of view: as a massive, uncontrolled and unasked-for food donation, especially for children (Borrel et al., 2001), and medicines lacking any coordination, with disastrous consequences in terms of redressing the costs for the mistakes made.

It was a long process featuring alternating phases, even in relation to the recurrence of emergencies in the Balkan area, and contradictory effects on the domestic scene: from a sort of illusion of power and ability to act – therefore one *can* mobilise help – which tends to put itself in motion and re-emerge as soon as the spotlights are on a new humanitarian emergency, to the construction of entrepreneurial abilities and new roles in the field of collecting support and funds to be used when needed – "useful" not only in relation to the potential beneficiaries but also for the acquisition of visibility and prestige of those who operate on the local and national scene.

This field is still evolving deeply and rapidly. Though the rhetoric and representation of the Balkan context have changed, in the passage to the phase of "development cooperation", currently in progress, other players have entered or are entering the field – for example businesses and their associative structures – thus creating new contexts and new problems, whose understanding appears important from both the theoretical and the practical viewpoint.

The Balkan scene as seen by the operators of Cooperazione Italiana
The impact with the context of ex-Yugoslavia immediately draws attention to the substantial inadequacy of the operational models used in previous experiences of international cooperation: an incompatibility of approaches that for many entailed a considerable period of decompression, of revision of acquired know-how and previous experiences.

As highlighted by many witnesses who operated in ex-Yugoslavia in various contexts and with different roles, coming from several field experiences in developing countries, not only Cooperazione Italiana, but "the entire international community projected itself in ex-Yugoslavia with the same attitude, which derived from the personal knowledge acquired in decades of work in developing countries. The community of donors had never before operated in a Western country, and we never would have imagined carrying out a humanitarian operation in Europe, to intervene *at home*" (Miozzo 1998, p. 24).

Following the collapse of a pre-existing welfare system, there were new health pathologies and new social problems relating to population targets not present in developing countries, such as the elderly; the existence of professionally prepared, European level counterparts made the dialogue difficult and demanding, as it entailed unusual requests for help, especially in the health field, not provided by any humanitarian aid protocols set at the developing countries' standard.

However, if on the one hand the fact of being European constituted an element of closeness and familiarity in relation to life contexts, on the other hand this vicinity hid the persistence of tangible differences on other levels. For instance, the long-lasting influence of realized socialism political and social institutions could be found in the widespread presence of bureaucratic-type working cultures, which were oriented towards executing tasks and not towards solving such complex problems as those caused by the post-war emergency: e.g. the need to manage great flows of money according to the logic imposed by international organs.

The impact with an essentially European context, even with its peculiar characteristics, immediately drew attention to this unmentioned yet evident aspect of every aid relationship: the logic of power inherent in the structure of aid itself.

For the first time, many operators coming from classic cooperation work circumstances and recruited to face the Yugoslav emergency found themselves operating in a context in which, also because of the high level of education characteristic of real socialist contexts, this asymmetry between donor and receiver was definitely not taken for granted. In this context, local players – who were socialised to forms of political participation, which, though different from those of liberal democracies, were nevertheless articulated and complex – expected the acknowledgement and the respect of institutional logic and formalised local powers that had certainly not been de-structured by the war emergency, and asked to check where aid wound up and to decide with their partners how to spend the money.

However, the request by local institutions representatives for a role of negotiation and decision-making on how to use the funds and to play an active part in their management, not only appeared to be unusual and difficult to set within the classic models of humanitarian intervention, but also implied the acceptance of local logic in the allocation of the resources, of their ways of conceiving democracy and "transparency", which were quite dissonant and considered absolutely unacceptable by those who operated according to the logic of international organisations.

In the representation of the institutional players who acted in this phase of humanitarian intervention, the complexity set by this unusual context entailed extenuating negotiations and the adoption of a strategy, deemed "necessary" at least in the first phase and in relation to the goals of "efficiency" imposed by the international organs of reference, based on employing the parlance and logic of humanitarian aid, which, as many authors have highlighted, involves a temporary suspension of sovereignty and a logic of substantial expropriation by including all local interlocutors in the category of "beneficiaries", by definition "vulnerable" and thus incapable of independent action and self-determination (Pandolfi 2002; Ignatieff 2002).

However, especially in Bosnia-Herzegovina where the intervention lasted much longer than the classic humanitarian ones, this strategy, which was easy to adopt in the phase of maximum emergency, was progressively replaced by different strategies centred more on the co-optation of local interlocutors within the projects.

However, the duration of the intervention entailed a progressive complexification of the context and the growing introduction of a different logic due to the converging action of different players: from the UN military humanitarian apparatus involved in territorial control, to the national diplomatic corps engaged in the definition and implementation of the Dayton Accords, to the NGOs, expression of all industrialised countries, and finally to what can be considered the new element of the Balkan experience, i.e. the entrance in the field, with forms and dimensions never seen before in past humanitarian crises, of volunteer associations, especially from Italy and other neighbouring European countries. As one of the witnesses underlines,

> "as it constitutes the first international crisis after the dissolution of the blocs, the Balkan experience represents an element of discontinuity, a divide between old and new emergencies: the dissolution of the blocs, in fact, broadening the capacity and possibility of intervention in areas no longer subject to protection, has multiplied and diversified policies of action making the areas of help contexts in which subjects with a market logic operate."

An arena where the offer of help has become, in time, diverse, as the request for aid is growingly differentiated, induced and attracted in part by the offer itself. An arena where the necessity is increasingly seized, unknown in interventions in developing countries, to create a network, to focus on the relationship with the other actors present on the scene, in order to understand their strategies, create alliances, avoid overlapping and position oneself on the aid market effectively.

And within this arena, characterised by growing complexity, unusual experiments are activated, new and often contradictory paths are pursued, conflicts have emerged and various types of negotiations have been opened, identities have been redefined and important phenomena of cultural hybridisation have been produced at different levels (Camerini, 1998; Canevaro, Berlini, Camasta, 1998).

Such complexity in perspective, according to many, seems bound to be reproduced in many contexts created by emergency interventions following natural and humanitarian catastrophes.

Conclusions

To conclude this reflection, I think it is important to highlight the role anthropology can and must play in offering analytical tools able to take into account the intertwining of elements and the complexity distinctive of new cooperation contexts.

In fact, besides the specific aim of any intervention, its realisation cannot leave aside the rebuilding and the analysis of the different contexts within which the action itself is articulated, as well as the local scenario where the object of the intervention is located.

In other words, the transnational character of the processes activated by both the new humanitarian crises and the development cooperation could be adequately studied and understood only through multi-local and multi-focused research strategies, which can highlight people's perceptions of their cultural milieu's transformations. At the same time, they will also allow to analyse the incidence of different yet interconnected issues in structuring the contexts of intervention: from local institutions to large organisations cutting national and regional borders transversally, from local cultures to the floods of information, imaginaries and meanings circulating within the media global system.

However, the critiques on applied anthropology made by development anthropology, though still barely accepted by those researchers personally involved in cooperation projects, have concretely contributed to enhancing their attention to the complexities due to the multiple actors present in the field, to the dynamics featuring the relationship between local contexts and the global world, to the virtual and real nomadism peculiar to the groups and individuals interacting with them and to their carrying out research mainly from an institutional and organisational specific location. This implies that they are objects of biased representations in terms of power from the beneficiaries of interventions.

Having abandoned the constrained and narrow perspective of an exclusive focus on the *local,* this anthropology has rebuilt the contact with the epistemological debate that crossed the discipline in the last two decades, and currently needs to rethink its objects of study, theoretical concepts and methodological approaches to be able to produce a knowledge that is functional to intervention within contexts characterised by a growing complexity (Gow, 2002).

References

AGIER, J.-M. (sous la dir. de) 1997: Anthropologues en danger. L'engagement sur le terrain. Paris: Michel Place.
APPADURAI, A. 1996: Modernity at Large: Cultural Dimension of Globalization. Mineapolis: University of Minnesota Press.
APPADURAI, A. 2002: Dead Certainty: Ethnic Violence in the Era of Globalisation. In: A. L. Hinton (ed.), Genocide: An Anthropological Reader. Malden: Blackwell Publishers.
BHABHA, H. 1994: The Location of Culture. London: Routledge.
BOROFSKY, R. 1994: Applying Anthropological Perspectives. In: R. Borofsky, Assessing Cultural Anthropology. New York: MacGraw-Hill.
BORREL, A., TAYLOR, A., MCGRATH, M., SEAL, A., HORMANN, E., PHELPS, L., MASON, F. 2001: From Policy to Practice: Challenges in Infant Feeding Emergencies during the Balkan Crisis. In: Disasters, vol. 25, n. 2.
BOTH, N. 2001: From Indifference to Entrapment: the Netherlands and the Yugoslav Crisis. In: International Affairs, vol. 77, n. 2.
CALLARI GALLI, M. 2000: Antropologia per insegnare. Milano: Bruno Mondadori.
CAMERINI, A. 1998: Aiutare ad aiutare: cooperativi in emergenza. In: A. Canevaro, M. G. Berlini, A. N. Camasta (eds,.), Pedagogia cooperativa in zone di guerra. Trento: Erikson.
CAMPBELL, D. 1999: Apartheid Cartography: the Political Anthropology and Spatial Effects of International Diplomacy in Bosnia. In: Political Geography, n. 18.
CANEVARO, A., BERLINI, M. G., CAMASTA, A. N., (eds.) 1998: Pedagogia cooperativa in zone di guerra. Trento: Erikson.
CARNIAWSKA, B. 1997: Narrating the Organization. Drama of Institutional Identity. Chicago: University of Chicago Press.
CERNEA, M. M. 1991: Knowledge from Social Science for Development Policies and Projects. In: M. M. Cernea (ed.), Putting People first: Sociological Variables in Rural Development. New York, Oxford: Oxford University Press.
CERNEA, M. M. 1995: Social Organization and Development Anthropology. In: Human Organization, n. 54.
CLIFFORD, J., MARCUS, G. E. (eds.) 1986: Writing Culture: Poetics and Politics of Ethnography. Berkeley: University of California Press.
COLAJANNI, A. 1998: Note sul futuro della professione antropologica: l'utilità dell'antropologia come problema teorico e applicativo. In: Etnoantropologia, n. 6–7
COLAJANNI, A. 1994: L'antropologia dello sviluppo in Italia. In: G. Di Cristofaro Longo, L. M. Lombardi Satriani (eds.), Gli Argonauti: l'antropologia e la società italiana. Roma: Armando.
ESCOBAR, A. 1991: Anthropology and the Development Encounter: the Making and Marketing of Development Anthropology. In: American Ethnologist, n. 18.

ESCOBAR, A. 1995: Encountering Development: the Making and Unmaking of the Third World. Princeton: Princeton University Press.

FABIETTI, U., 1999: Antropologia culturale. L'esperienza e l'interpretazione. Bari: Laterza.

FABIETTI, U., 2000: Il traffico delle culture. In: U. Fabietti, R. Malighetti, V. Matera, Dal tribale al globale. Milano: Bruno Mondadori.

FISHER, W. F. 1997: DOING GOOD? The Politics and Antipolitics of NGO Practice. In: Annual Review of Anthropology, n. 23.

GOW, D. D. 2002: Anthropology and Development: Evil Twin or Moral Narrative. In: Human Organization, vol. 61, n. 4.

GRILLO, R. D., REW, A. (eds.) 1985: Social Anthropology and Development Policy. London: Tavistock.

GRILLO, R., RICCIO, B. 2004: Translocal Development: Italy-Senegal. In: Population, Space and Place 10, 99–111.

HANNERZ, U. 1992: Cultural Complexity: Studies in the Social Organization of Meaning. New York: Columbia University Press.

HANNERZ, U. 1996: Transnational Connections. Culture, People, Places. London-New York: Routledge.

HAYDEN, R. M. 2002: Imagined Communities and Real Victims: Self-Determination and Ethnic Cleasing in Yugoslavia. In: A. L. Hinton, Genocide: An Anthropological Reader. Malden: Blackwell Publishers.

HOBEN, A. 1982: Anthropologists and Development. In: Annual Review of Anthropology, vol. 11.

HUDSON, A. 2001: NGOs' Transnational Advocacy Networks: from "Legitimacy" to "Political responsibility"? In: Global Networks, vol. 1, n. 4.

HYMES, D. (ed.) 1999 [1969]: Reinventing Anthropology. Chicago: University of Michigan Press.

IANNI, V. 1999: La cooperazione decentrata allo sviluppo umano. Torino: Rosemberg & Sellier.

IGNATIEFF, M. 2002: Intervention and State Failure. In: Dissent, vol. 49.

LEWIS, D. 1999: Revealing, Widening, Deepening? A Review of the Existing and Potential Contribution of Anthropological Approaches to the "Third Sector". In: Human Organization, vol. 58, n. 1.

MALIGHETTI, R. 2002: Post-colonialismo e post-sviluppo: l'attualità dell'antropologia coloniale. In: Antropologia, n. 22.

MARKOWITZ, L. 2001: Finding the Field: Notes on the Ethnography of NGOs. In: Human Organization, vol. 60, n. 1.

MATTIOLI, S. 1999: Mi piace che siano misti. Pesaro: Magma edizioni.

METHA, L. 2001: The World Bank and Its Emerging Knowledge Empire. In: Human Organization, vol. 60, n. 2.

MIOZZO, A. 1998: Cosa è Cooperazione Italiana. In: A. Canevaro, M. G. Berlini, A. N. Camasta (eds.), 1998, Pedagogia cooperativa in zone di guerra. Trento: Erikson.

NAGENGAST, C. 1994: Violence, Terror and the Crisis of the State. In: Annual Review of Anthropology, vol. 23.

NOLAN, R. W. 2002: Development Anthropology: Encounters in the Real World. Boulder, Co.: Westview Press.

PANDOLFI, M 2000: L'industrie humanitaire: une souveraineté mouvante et supra-coloniale. Réflexion sul l'experience des Balkans. In: Multitudes, Automne 2000.

PANDOLFI, M. 2002: "Moral Entrepreneurs", souverainetés mouvantes et barbelées: la bio-politique dans les Balkans postcommunistes. In: Anthropologie et Société, vol. 26, n. 1.

SABELLI, F. 1993, Recherche anthropologique et développement. Neuchatel: Editions de l'Institut d'Ethnologie, Paris: Maison de sciences de l'homme.

TOMMASOLI, M. 2001: Lo sviluppo partecipativo. Analisi sociale e logiche di pianificazione. Roma: Carocci.

Authors

Matilde Callari Galli
is Professor of Cultural Anthropology at the Department of Sciences of Education, University of Bologna. She has been president of AISEA (Italian Association of Ethno-Anthropological Sciences: 1995-1998). Her research interests include: Anthropology of Education; Anthropology of Human Rights; Urban Anthropology; Anthropology of Tourism; Media and Women Studies. She has published numerous books and articles. Amongst her most recent publications: the co-edited book (with Giovanna Guerzoni and Bruno Riccio) *Culture e conflitto* (Guaraldi: 2005), the volume *Antropologia senza confini* (Sellerio: 2005) and the forthcoming *Mappe urbane* (Guaraldi: 2007). Correspondence to: Dipartimento di Scienze dell'Educazione "Giovanni Maria Bertin"; via Filippo Re, 6; 40126 Bologna; Italia; e-mail: matilde.callari@unibo.it.

Zelda Alice Franceschi
teaches Cultural Anthropology at the Faculty of Letters and Philosophy, University of Bologna. She received her PHD from the University of Milan "Bicocca" (2002) and her research interests include: Life history; Biography; Memory; Identity. She is currently undertaking fieldwork among the Wichí community in the Chaco region (Argentina). She has published numerous articles and the monograph *Storie di vita. Percorsi nella storia dell'Antropologia Americana*, (Clueb: 2006). Correspondance to: Dipartimento di Discipline Storiche; Piazza San Giovanni in Monte, 2; e-mail: zelda.franceschi@unibo.it.

Ivo Giuseppe Pazzagli
is Researcher and Lecturer in Cultural Anthropology at the Department of Sciences of Education, University of Bologna. His research interests include: Anthropology of Education; Anthropology of Organizations and Policies; Tourism; Aid and Development. He has published numerous articles in journals and edited books and he is the editor of the Anthropological series for the publisher Guaraldi in which his edited book *I nuovi territori dell'identità* (2007) is forthcoming. Correspondence to: Dipartimento di Scienze dell'Educazione "Giovanni Maria Bertin"; via Filippo Re, 6; 40126 Bologna; Italia; e-mail: ivogiuseppe.pazzagli@unibo.it.

Bruno Riccio
is Researcher and Lecturer in Cultural Anthropology at the Department of Education, University of Bologna. He received a D.Phil from the University of Sussex (2000) and his research interests include: Anthropology of Migration, Multiculturalism and Racism; Translocal Co-development; Tourism; Urban Anthropology. He has published numerous articles and edited volumes. Amongst his re-

cent publications: an edited issue on "African migrants in Italy" (2005) for the journal *afriche e orienti* and the book *Toubab e vu cumprà: transnazionalità e rappresentazioni nelle migrazioni senegalesi in Italia* (Cleup: 2007). Correspondence to: Dipartimento di Scienze dell'Educazione "Giovanni Maria Bertin"; via Filippo Re, 6; 40126 Bologna; Italia; e-mail: bruno.riccio@unibo.it.

Luigi Urru
Studied at the School of Oriental and African Studies (SOAS) and received a PHD in Anthropology from the University of Milan "Bicocca" (2002) where he is currently teaching Anthropology of Contemporary Japan. He has been Canon Foundation Fellow and Visiting Researcher at the Jinnai Laboratory of Architecture, University Hôsei, Tokyo (2003) and Japan Foundation Trainee (2005). His book *Il fantasma tra i ciliegi. Topografie di primavera a Tokyo* is forthcoming with the publisher Liguori. Correspondence to: via Bertholet, 2; 10125 Torino; Italia; e-mail: luigiurru@hotmail.com.

Freiburger Sozialanthropologische Studien

hrsg. von Christian Giordano (Universität Fribourg, Schweiz) in Verbindung mit Edouard Conte (Universität Bern), Dobrinka Kostova (Bulgarische Akademie der Wissenschaften, Sofia), Véronique Pache Huber (Universität Fribourg, Schweiz) Klaus Roth (Universität München), François Rüegg (Universität Fribourg, Schweiz)

Christian Giordano; Jean-Luc Patry (Hg.)
Theorie und Praxis – Brüche und Brücken
Seit der Mensch denkt (d. h. seit er theoretisiert), besteht ein Bruch zwischen Theorie und Praxis. In fast allen Disziplinen spielt der Gegensatz zwischen der grauen Theorie und dem grünen oder goldenen Leben (der Praxis) eine wesentliche Rolle. Wie sieht dieser Bruch genau aus, und wie kann man ihn überbrücken? Diese Fragen wurden von international ausgewiesenen Experten aus diversen Disziplinen (Erziehungswissenschaft, Psychologie, Sprachwissenschaften, Theologie, Philosophie, Kommunikationswissenschaft und Sozialanthropologie) diskutiert und die Ergebnisse sind im vorliegenden Band zusammengetragen. Trotz der unterschiedlichen Disziplinen und der individuellen Vorgangsweisen zeigt sich immer wieder, dass der Abstand zwischen Theorie und Praxis zwar verringert, aber nie aufgelöst werden kann, dass Brücken zwar geschlagen werden, letztlich aber der Einzelne (sei er Praktiker oder Theoretiker) den Weg von der einen zur anderen Seite selber gehen muss. Jede Disziplin hat dazu ihre eigenen Vorgangsweisen, ja in der gleichen Disziplin können diese sehr unterschiedlich sein. Aber niemals ist der Bruch ein vollständiger, immer gibt es Brücken und Wege – man muss sie nur (er-)finden.
Bd. 10, 2006, 168 S., 19,90 €, br., ISBN 3-8258-9068-6

Barbara Furrer
Der Alltag politischer Institutionen
Repräsentationen und Praktiken im Schweizer Bundesparlament
Die vorliegende Studie beleuchtet das Funktionieren des Schweizer Bundesparlaments als politische Institution aus einer politisch-anthropologischen Perspektive – ein Thema, das im Fach Sozialanthropologie bisher wenig beachtet wurde. Der Akzent wird auf die konkreten Performanzen der sozialen Akteurinnen und Akteure gesetzt. Mit theoretischen Überlegungen zu den Konzepten „Institution", „Praktiken", „Herrschaft" und „Legitimität" wird an Hand empirischer Daten gezeigt, dass die alltagsparlamentarischen Handlungsvollzüge der Erhaltung und Erlangung von Herrschaftspositionen dienen, und dass die sozialen Repräsentationen zur politischen Produktion von Legitimität führen.
Bd. 11, 2006, 168 S., 19,90 €, br., ISBN 3-8258-9339-1

Helza Lanz
Flexible Persistenz
Dezentralisierung und Handlungsraionalität in Brasilien
Abbau von Staatlichkeit, Erhöhung der Effizienz und Entscheidungsfreiräume für die lokalen politischen Landschaft scheinen heutzutage das goldene Rezept für ein neues Regierungsmodell darzustellen. Der Bundesstaat Ceará gilt in Brasilien als Vorreiter der Dezentralisierungsbestrebungen, die als Antwort auf das Scheitern der staatszentralistischen Entwicklungsmodelle wiederbelebt wurden. Diese Studie, basierend auf anthropologischen Feldforschung, untersucht wie innovativ und wie weit diese Tendenzen zu einer verstärkten sozialen Integration führen. Die brasilianische Gesellschaft ist ein hervorragendes Beispiel für die ungeheure Widerstandskraft der Sozialstrukturen gegen alle bisherigen Reformversuche. Die Autorin geht den Gründen für die Persistenz der Sozialstrukturen nach, um die Kohärenz und Rationalität der Hand-

lungsstrategien der Brasilianer verstehend zu rekonstruieren.
Bd. 13, 2006, 256 S., 29,90 €, br.,
ISBN 3-8258-9759-1

Barbara Waldis; Reginald Byron (Eds.)
Migration and Marriage
Heterogamy and Homogamy in a Changing World
In a world in which migration and the mixing of peoples are increasing while at the same time multicultural ideology has given rise to the reassertion of putative primordial differences between peoples, interesting questions are raised about the relationships between political rhetoric and social action, groupness and individuality, and the public and the private. The rate of intermarriage is considered by sociologists the most important statistical test of the strength or weakness of structural divisions within societies. What do social anthropologists have to say about heterogamy and homogamy in situations of movement and flux, and what does this tell us about processes of boundary-definition?
Bd. 14, 2006, 224 S., 24,90 €, br.,
ISBN 3-8258-9873-3

Klaus Roth (Hg.)
Arbeit im Sozialismus – Arbeit im Postsozialismus
Erkundungen zum Arbeitsleben im östlichen Europa
Bd. 1, 2004, 440 S., 39,90 €, br.,
ISBN 3-8258-7374-9

Véronique Pache Huber
Le mariage de l'Amour et de la Raison
Stratégies matrimoniales de la classe moyenne en Inde
Bd. 2, 2004, 288 S., 29,90 €, br.,
ISBN 3-8258-7865-1

Josef Siegen
Re-konstruierte Vergangenheit
Das Lötschental und das Durnholzertal. Wirtschaftliche und sozio-kulturelle Entwicklung von zwei abgeschlossenen Alpentälern zwischen 1920 und 2000 aus der Sicht der Betroffenen
Bd. 3, 2005, 424 S., 39,90 €, br.,
ISBN 3-8258-8041-9

Klaus Roth (Hg.)
Arbeitswelt – Lebenswelt
Facetten einer spannungsreichen Beziehung im östlichen Europa
Bd. 4, 2006, 256 S., 29,90 €, br.,
ISBN 3-8258-8060-5

Monica Budowski
Does Dignity Matter?
Daily Practice of Lone Mothers in Costa Rica
Bd. 5, 2005, 296 S., 29,90 €, br.,
ISBN 3-8258-8072-9

Christian Giordano; Jean-Luc Patry (Hg.)
Wertkonflikte und Wertewandel
Eine pluridisziplinäre Begegnung
Bd. 6, 2005, 168 S., 19,90 €, br.,
ISBN 3-8258-8073-7

Michel Streith
Dynamiques paysannes en Mecklembourg
Survie d'un savoir-faire
Bd. 7, 2005, 232 S., 29,90 €, br.,
ISBN 3-8258-8074-5

François Rüegg; Rudolf Poledna; Calin Rus (Eds.)
Interculturalism and Discrimination in Romania
Policies, Practices, Identities and Representations
Bd. 8, 2006, 344 S., 24,90 €, br.,
ISBN 3-8258-8075-3

Ivan Čolović
Le Bordel des Guerriers
Folklore, politique et guerre
Bd. 9, 2005, 160 S., 19,90 €, br.,
ISBN 3-8258-8076-1

LIT Verlag GmbH & Co. KG Wien – Zürich
Auslieferung Österreich: Medienlogistik Pichler-ÖBZ GmbH & Co KG
IZ-NÖ Süd, Straße 1, Objekt 34, A-2355 Wiener Neudorf, Postfach 133
Tel. +43 (0) 2236/63 535 - 290, Fax +43 (0) 2236/63 535 - 243, e-Mail: bestellen@medien-logistik.at
Auslieferung Deutschland: Fresnostr. 2 48159 Münster
Tel.: 0251 – 62 03 222 – Fax 0251 – 23 19 72
e-Mail: vertrieb@lit-verlag.de – http://www.lit-verlag.de